BRUISED
BUT NOT
BROKEN

BRUISED
BUT NOT
BROKEN

STANLEY C. BALDWIN

MULTNOMAH
Portland, Oregon 97266

Cover design and illustration by Al Mendenhall
Edited by Steve Halliday

BRUISED BUT NOT BROKEN
© 1985 by Multnomah Press
Portland, Oregon 97266

Printed in the United States of America

Library of Congress Cataloging in Publication Data

Baldwin, Stanley C.
    Bruised but not broken.

    1. Christian life—1960-   2. Consolation.
I. Title.
BV4501.2.B3818   1985   248.4   85-2977
ISBN 0-88070-080-7 (pbk.)

    92 93 94 95 96 97 98 99 - 10 9 8 7 6 5 4 3 2

Contents

Foreword

This is a wonderful book. After all the "how-to" and "can-do" volumes that have been filling the shelves of Christian bookstores, it is a relief to read someone who can identify with our real situations and tell it the way it is. Stanley Baldwin is a friend who talks with us in nontechnical ways about the things that matter most to us—the things that keep us from the Christian victory stand. As he says, the real reason that the Christian rejoices is not that he has come through triumphantly, but that God is always with us to strengthen us.

The incidents and illustrations here related are taken from real life. People are frustrated; people fail; people become victims of illness; people die. Yet God is there, and that's what we want to hear. That's the encouragement we need.

Miracles are dandy, but God is better. He won't let us down.

Mr. Baldwin is a Christian writer who helps people. The hard places will still be there after you have read this book. But you will have the joy of this assurance: you are not alone. That's not much of a cushion, but it is a great lift to the morale. And it is morale—not aspirin—that wins the battles of life, morale that is solidly based on the fruit of the Spirit.

Recently I was in a prayer meeting and discovered that two of those present were afraid to go home that night. Dig underneath the pleasant smiles of most folks and you will find deep, deep hurts. For all such, a thoughtful perusal of these chapters will spell recognition, identity, and genuine appreciation. My congratulations to both author and publisher.

Sherwood Eliot Wirt

Part 1

Getting Squared Away with God Again

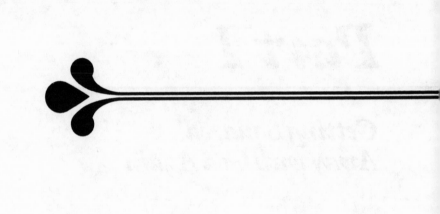

1
When It Seems God Has Failed You

A Promising Ministry

Robert Foster and his wife Jane had been called to a small, struggling church. It was Bob's first pastorate. The church could only offer a small salary, well below what the government called the poverty level. Of course, as the church grew, so would Bob's salary. In the meantime, he and Jane would have to "trust the Lord."

After much prayer, the Fosters accepted the call. They believed they were stepping out on the promise of God. One verse especially summed it up: "My God will meet all your needs according to his glorious riches in Christ Jesus" (Philippians 4:19).

Bob launched into his new ministry enthusiastically. The people were responsive and their numbers began to grow.

Then the mill—the town's chief economic support—began cutting back. One of Bob's best men was laid off and announced plans to move away.

Bob and Jane winced, but held on; they had come by faith and were not about to give up. Still, there were bills to pay, a car to keep running and insured, two small children who needed food, clothing, vitamins, doctor's visits, and maybe an occasional trip to McDonald's.

Six months later Bob and Jane looked back on those hard times as "the good old days." The mill curtailment that everyone hoped would be short-lived was shorter than anyone wanted. Now the mill would close altogether.

The church no longer had the resources to support a full-time pastor and his family. Bob and Jane were beaten. They would have to leave.

"It took us several years to get over that," they said recently. "Not just the trauma of being poor. Worse than that was the blow to our faith. We had counted on what we thought was God's promise, and we had been let down. How could we ever again be sure of his promises?"

Disappointed Faith

Like Bob and Jane, many Christians have somehow had their faith disappointed. This experience should be distinguished from merely facing difficulty or suffering. Hard as that may be, it should not be unexpected. Jesus told us that in this world we would have tribulation (see John 16:33). What's harder is to believe that God has promised us something . . . and then he fails to come through.

Disappointments to faith can occur in many different settings. Consider a few more actual cases.

The Child Who Strays

Esther is sure her little boy Eric will grow up to know and love the Lord. She claims God's promise, "Train a child in the way he should go, and when he is old he will not turn from it" (Proverbs 22:6).

Esther has been through one unsuccessful marriage and a divorce, but that was before she knew the Lord. Now middle-aged, she is an ardent Christian. Eric is the only child of her second marriage. Esther is determined that things will turn out right with Eric. She has claimed him for God.

Sue, Esther's cousin of about the same age, has been a pastor's wife for years. She tells Esther that her son will ultimately make his own choice about following the Lord. No matter what Esther does, it's possible that Eric may turn away from God. Sue has seen things like that happen. She is concerned that Esther's own faith may collapse if or when Eric strays. Not that she'd be likely to renounce Christ; but she might well join the ranks of the walking wounded and alienate herself from her Lord.

Esther doesn't come right out and say so, but she suggests that those parents whose children have strayed from God must have failed somewhere along the line. Sue admits it. Of course they have failed, all parents do. Nevertheless, Sue insists that even good parents who train their children "in the way they should go" sometimes experience heartbreak as they see their children turn from God.

Esther remains unshaken. She has God's promise. "God said it, I believe it, and that settles it," she declares.

But life has a way of "unsettling" things. In this case it remains to be seen whether Esther is right. But there certainly are some parents who once echoed her convictions, only to find out the hard way that they were wrong.

The Healing That Never Comes

A hundred miles away from where Esther is claiming her son for God, a woman named Francine also claimed a divine promise.

Francine was a delightful, warm-hearted woman, aged thirty-nine. She loved the Lord and she loved people. She was the spiritual sparkplug of her family. Though her husband and three almost-grown children were Christians, it was Francine who glowed for God.

Even after grim-faced doctors diagnosed her "gall bladder problem" as liver cancer and gave her ten weeks to live, Francine remained positive. She believed in the healing power of God. Far more than affirming that God *could* heal her, Francine believed he *would*.

As she prayed and studied the scriptural promises, Francine became even more certain of her healing. For her to die made no sense. Her family needed her. She was a key witness for Christ in a dark community. She was still young. Surely this sickness was an attack of Satan.

Francine got some teaching tapes that encouraged her to "name it and claim it." Whatever she would ask in Jesus' name, believing, it would be granted. The Word of God said so (see Matthew 21:22; John 14:13).

The ten weeks allotted by her doctors came and went with Francine still very much alive. She reported at a church service that she'd had a vision from the Lord. In the vision she had seen herself completely healed.

So despite the yellow color of her skin that betrayed a diseased liver, Francine kept "naming and claiming" her healing.

Then about eighteen months after she became ill, Francine noticed one day that her stools had turned white. She knew what that meant—the disease had proceeded to the point of no return. Her liver damage was irreversible. She could not live.

Francine wept out her fear and disappointment to a close friend, but then resumed her "naming and claiming." There were preparations for death that Francine needed to make, but couldn't, because she was "going to be healed." Her family, following her example, treated her almost as if she were not sick. Longstanding problems between Francine and her children continued unresolved just as they had for years.

Toward the end, she became too weak to deal with the questions *why?* and *what happened to God's promise?*

About two years after she became ill, Francine died.
Her husband and children haven't been to church since.

The Equal Yoke that Breaks

Michelle is a young mother of four children. Her first husband walked out on her four years ago. Since then, Michelle has come to know the Lord and has found a whole new life in Christ.

Like most other single parents, Michelle entertained hopes of one day marrying again. Her church taught that as the innocent party, Michelle was free to remarry, only "in the Lord." That meant she should definitely marry a man who shared her faith in Christ. It also meant that she needed to marry in God's will.

"We know it's hard to wait, but God will bless you for it," her friends said.

Michelle had made a firm commitment to Christ as Lord and wasn't about to compromise that now by marrying unwisely. She gave the whole matter to the Lord in prayer.

Two years later Michelle walked down the aisle, her heart almost bursting with joy. She had honored the Lord, and now he had given her a Christian man with whom to share the rest of her life.

Today Michelle is alone again with her four children. She lives on welfare.

Her husband walked out on her.

The Search for Answers

What can we say to these things? How shall we help those who have been disappointed when they acted on their faith in God's promises? Are the promises of God to be trusted?

Let's consider some answers often suggested. Perhaps each one is at least partially correct.

1. *The promises don't fail, people do.*

Perhaps the most common reaction Christians have to another's disappointed faith is suspicion (or even accusation). "Let God be true, and every man a liar" expresses this view (see Romans 3:4). If your faith was disappointed, you must have failed to meet the conditions; that's all there is to it. If a child goes astray, he wasn't truly trained up in the way he should go. If a pastor was driven out by lack of funds, he must have given up too easily, lacked faith, or failed somehow. If a sick person was not healed, he must have lacked faith or misinterpreted the promises in the first place. If a woman's marriage fails twice, she must harbor some grievous fault.

Maybe so. Sometimes people do fail God and then blame him for failing them. But to say that is true in a specific case can be both judgmental and cruel. It places us in the company of Job's accusers. They were sure Job was responsible somehow for the calamities that befell him. In their view, either God or Job was at fault. Since they were not about to blame God, that left Job as the only candidate.

They were wrong.

2. *The promises are "spiritual," not literal.*

With a little imagination almost all of God's promises can be explained away. Does the Bible say, "My God shall supply all your needs"? (Philippians 4:19, NASB). Yes, but what does a Christian really need? We don't need anything, some say, except Jesus. We don't need money, cars, houses, lands, food, health. We don't even need to survive here on earth. We have all in Jesus.

One preacher went so far as to claim that this is why the verse (in many versions) says God will supply your *need* rather than your *needs;* your only need is Jesus.

The many promises that prayer will be answered can be dealt with handily by a similar spiritualizing. People pray for a sick person to get well; they claim the relevant promises. Then when the patient dies someone says, "He has received his perfect healing. He has gone to be with the Lord, where there is no more sickness or pain."

If it's prosperity that is promised, one can say, "Well, we may be poor in this world's goods, but we are rich in heavenly things."

This approach is not wholly wrong. No doubt some have "claimed" promises that God never made, or they have misunderstood and misapplied a legitimate one. We parents should understand this well, because our own children often read into our remarks ironclad promises that we never intended.

"Can we go to the beach next Saturday? Please, Mommy?"

"Well, maybe, if it's a nice day."

Saturday dawns bright and clear, and before Mommy is even wide awake the child is excitedly preparing to go to the beach.

"We *can't* go, dear," Mommy explains. "The car's broken down."

"But you promised! Waaaah."

It's possible to read into another's words more than was intended. Is it possible we sometimes do that with God?

On the other hand, explaining away God's promises in this fashion can also be a cop-out. When Paul said that God would supply all our need, did he mean that our only need is Jesus? No! The context speaks about material needs. The Christians at Philippi sent a gift to Paul out of concern for him, and in return Paul wanted to assure them that God would provide for their needs as well.

Maybe some promises are to be taken "spiritually," but we also need to remember the old maxim: "Those who have spiritual eyes don't spiritualize and thereby tell spiritual lies."

3. *The "promises" are general statements of fact or are*

specific promises to others; they are not necessarily personal guarantees to us.

"Train a child in the way he should go, and when he is old he will not turn from it." This is no guarantee from God that your child, if he is trained properly in the Christian faith, will be a Christian. It is rather a general observation about the nature of life. Childhood training will ordinarily have a lasting and decisive effect on a person.

Some point out that the saying is, after all, a proverb, and is identified as such in the text (see Proverbs 10:1). It is a saying much like, "A rolling stone gathers no moss," or "A stitch in time saves nine." Should you happen to find moss on a rolling stone, you would not therefore enter a crisis of faith, reject the proverb's validity, and doubt the integrity of the one who spoke it. Should a stitch in time prove wasted on occasion because the whole fabric is rotten, that would not invalidate the proverb.

Other promises, one might argue, are like the assurance Paul gave the Philippians that their needs would be supplied. This was addressed to them, not to us.

While there is validity to the argument that not everything in the Bible applies directly to us, we'd lose virtually the whole book if we never acted on anything originally addressed to someone else.

So how do we decide whether a biblical promise is ours to claim personally and literally? That's a tough question. We don't want to be among those who do not have because we do not ask. But neither do we want to end up doubting God—or secretly angry at him—because we have assumed too much.

My own answer is that if a humble study of the Scriptures plus the inner witness of the Spirit leads me to believe a promise is for me, then I claim it. But even when I do so, I try to *center my faith supremely in the Promiser rather than in the promise.* There is a difference!

Faith in Formulas

Something about human nature loves formulas. We want predictability, regularity, uniformity. This desire isn't bad. There is order in the universe. Science would be impossible if everything behaved randomly, if there were no "promise" that a given set of conditions would produce a given result.

Our trouble is that we sometimes try to put God in our little boxes. We want predictable, regular, and uniform behavior from him. Within very large parameters, even this is okay. God is love and we must expect that he will predictably, regularly, and uniformly act on the basis of love.

But that doesn't mean we can predict what specific action he will take in a given case. Paul knew that: "O the depth of the riches both of the wisdom and knowledge of God! how unsearchable are His judgments, and His ways past finding out!" (Romans 11:33, KJV).

Though God's ways are "past finding out," we continue to imagine that we have found them out. Based on this arrogant assumption, we proceed to predict what God will do—and sometimes what he *must* do. If he fails to salute sometime when we raise our flag, suddenly there's a crisis.

It seems that we want God to put his omnipotence to work in our situation, but we don't want his omniscience—we think we already know enough ourselves.

Job found that God didn't always act according to his expectations, nor according to those of his contemporaries. Still he was able to say, "Though he slay me, yet will I hope in him" (Job 13:15). He could no longer say, "I trust this or that will be the outcome," but he could still say, "I trust in him."

There is a song I used to take exception to every time I heard it. The song expressed a strong determination to go on believing in God no matter what. It said something to the effect that even if the sun and moon stopped shining and no miracle were ever seen again, the singer would still trust in the Lord.

I thought, *No, that sounds good, but it's an exaggeration. If the sun and moon ceased to shine, that would prove God untrue, because he said they would shine until the end of time* (see Genesis 8:22).

Now I've decided the song is right. It still sounds like an implicit contradiction of Scripture, and I fully expect to see both the sun and the moon shining until Jesus comes. But if they don't, I'll still believe. My faith is in God, not in some conditions I understand him to have promised.

Celebrating God

Many martyrs have given their lives for the cause of Christ, and reading of them is no particular test of faith for most believers. We don't wrestle with questions about how God could have allowed it. Jesus forewarned his followers to expect persecution. We are not surprised at anything the world might do to Christians.

One particular incident, however, seems disturbingly different. These men died, not at the hands of an enemy, but because "God let them starve."

Perhaps I'm especially fascinated with Captain Allen Gardiner because the last dramatic chapter of his life began on my birthday, December 17. It was on that date, though back in 1850, that Gardiner and six intrepid companions landed at Patagonia on the southern tip of South America. Their task was to take the gospel to a people so primitive that the evolutionist Charles Darwin had said they existed "in a lower state . . . than in any other part of the world."

Gardiner, a seasoned captain of the British navy, had made careful preparations for their mission. He had twice before visited the area, once staying for three months. He knew the natives to be treacherous cannibals and the land and weather to be severe.

He took with him two double-deck launches, the *Pioneer* and the *Speedwell,* and six-months' supply of provisions. His team included a medical doctor and a ship's carpenter. In England he had a group of supporters who were to send him a second six-months' supply of goods.

On December 18 Gardiner said goodbye to the *Ocean Queen,* the ship that had carried his party from England. "Nothing can exceed the cheerful endurance and unanimity of the whole party," he wrote. "I feel that the Lord is with us, and cannot doubt that he will own and bless the work which he has permitted us to begin."

The very next month Gardiner's supporters in England began seeking a ship to carry the next six-months' provisions to Patagonia. No one would risk it. Can you imagine the thoughts of the missionaries as day after day they searched the horizon for a ship that never came? Could the tempter have passed up such an opportunity to question the love and faithfulness of Almighty God?

Fighting scurvy, cold, and hunger, plus the hostility of those they had come to win, the little band must have known some dark days of discouragement.

In October of 1851, when a relief ship finally reached Patagonia, the horrified crew found the missionaries dead of starvation. Gardiner's body, clad in three suits and with wool stockings over his arms to ward off the numbing cold, was found lying beside a boat. In his journal was a record of the ordeal. At one point Gardiner wrote:

> Poor and weak as we are, our boat is very
> Bethel to our souls, for we feel and know
> that God is here. Asleep or awake, I am,
> beyond the power of expression, happy.

God did not supply his physical needs. He and his companions had sought first the kingdom of God, but the material things had not been added unto them. Still, while he could not say God's provision was there, he could and did say, "God is here."

I do not know whether Captain Gardiner or his men ever wondered if God had failed them. If they did, there was no hint of it in his last communication. It was dated September 6, 1851, almost nine months after his arrival in Patagonia and only about a month before help arrived.

> Yet a little while and though . . . (obliterated) the Almighty to sing the praises . . . throne. I neither hunger nor thirst, though five days without food . . .

Eight years later the society Gardiner had founded sent a second mission to Patagonia. The natives attacked, killing all but one of the party.

Two years after that a third effort resulted in a permanent station, and after four years more, the first baptisms. Eventually a boat was commissioned to work all along the coast, taking the gospel to the natives; its name, the *Allen Gardiner*.

At last even Charles Darwin acknowledged his admiration for the results. "The success of the mission," he wrote, "is most wonderful and charms me, as I always prophesied utter failure. I shall feel proud if your committee think fit to elect me an honorary member of your society."

Can we trust God to keep his promises?

We cannot be sure God will always do what we think he should. David wrote, "I was young and now I am old, yet I have never seen the righteous forsaken or their children begging bread" (Psalm 37:25). But David never knew Allen Gardiner, did he?

Nevertheless, God does take care of his own. If in his divine wisdom he sees fit to make an exception to some general rule, we should say, "Let God be God."

Yes, we can trust God to keep his promises. More than that, *we can trust God.*

He is the King of the universe, the all-knowing

Sovereign, the Almighty. He has said he loves us . . . and he sent his only Son to prove it.

And *that* is a God to be trusted!

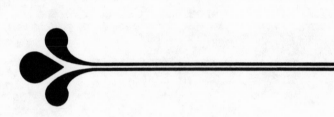

2
When You Know You Have Failed God

205 Pounds Of Guilt

Betty Hunt had finally reached the end. Not the bottom—she had been there a long time. Almost all her life. As a child she was ashamed of herself, of her poor parents, of her clothes, of wetting her pants, of being fat, of having no friends.

There had been hope briefly in her teens. A foster family had taken her to church and she had responded to the message of salvation through Christ. To get love, she could accept even the strict standards of the home—including no shows and no dances. But when she felt unaccepted there, when she knew she was still second-rate, she turned from God.

She married early—a man whose parents thought she wasn't good enough for their son. She proved them right. While he was away in the navy, she had affairs with other men. After they divorced, she left him with both of their children so she would not have the responsibility. Not that she would give up her fast life of drink and men to take care of them anyhow; but this was simpler.

Betty spent the next years as a promiscuous drunk in

a life of hell on earth. She drank so she wouldn't have to think about what a rotten person she was. And she used men both to feel loved and to hurt the men.

Her daughter, at age thirteen, came back into Betty's life. Unwanted by her father, the girl had idolized her absent mother and moved in adoring her. Within a month Betty had turned her into a scared, angry, bitter girl ready for the streets.

By this time Betty had been "dried out" at every hospital in the city and owed so many bills that neither the hospitals nor the ambulance companies would serve her anymore. They had given up on her and told her so. "If you want to kill yourself, we can't stop you," they said.

Betty had been in state hospitals for the cure. She had been in Alcoholics Anonymous and had stayed dry for one year. Several times she had tried to kill herself with an overdose of drugs and alcohol. She had been in a coma once for twenty-seven hours, and the doctors had predicted she would die or become a vegetable.

Now at age thirty-eight she was at the end. She couldn't drink any more and live, but she couldn't stop, either. She got on her knees. "God, I can't take it anymore," she prayed.

That was four years ago, and Betty Hunt hasn't had a drink since. "God gave me sobriety," she says. "There is no other explanation. I didn't imagine it would be easy and it wasn't. But I felt I had a promise from the Lord and he would always be there and that together we could make it."

The desire to die left Betty immediately. Before, she had been terrified of death, even though she didn't want to live. She felt unworthy of life, and that was one reason she drank. Now she began overcoming a lifelong weight problem also, going from 205 pounds to 125.

Other remarkable things began to happen. Before, she had been a people-pleaser, trying to be what others wanted so they would accept her. At the same time, she had been a people-hater, deliberately hurting others out of her own pain and anger.

Now God began showing her how destructive all of this was. She could not be what others wanted—and she didn't need to be. She could only be who she was. She didn't have to hurt others, either.

God also turned her guilt around. She'd had plenty of guilt, and she drank so as not to feel it. Now God had forgiven her. Christ had died for all her sins. She felt pain over what she had done, especially as she saw the effects in her daughter and son. Sometimes the guilt would threaten to come surging back. Betty knew she couldn't allow it to engulf her, or it would send her right back to drink. All she could do was live responsibly toward her daughter and son and everyone else from now on.

So here was another paradox. Feeling guilty over all her wrongdoing only made her do worse, while feeling forgiven made her do better. That's a principle many people have yet to understand, but it's a consistent message of the Bible.

Let's consider, then, what it means to fail God, and what the Bible says to those of us who have done so.

I've Let God Down

Richard Nixon lost the presidency of the United States over Watergate. He was the only president in history to resign the office. Had he not done so, he almost certainly would have been impeached.

For years afterward, Nixon was asked why he would not—then or since—simply confess his wrong and ask the forgiveness of the American people. His response was that he would not grovel.

The former president did, however, confess with apparent pain that he had "let down" his family, his friends and supporters, and the American people. It obviously hurt him to feel and know that he had so grievously failed those who had trusted him.

One of the most devastating things that can happen to any of us is to feel and know that we have let down God. Strong men weep over it. The cries of such people are among the most heart-wrenching words in Scripture.

One strong man especially comes to mind.

Peter told the Lord that he would never let him down, not even if he had to die for him. Soon afterward, he denied three times that he was a disciple of Jesus. We read that "The Lord turned and looked straight at Peter. Then Peter remembered the word the Lord had spoken to him: 'Before the rooster crows today, you will disown me three times.' And he went outside and wept bitterly" (Luke 22:61-62).

Failing the Lord was too much for him to bear.

Trouble from Within

Until now in this book we have considered things that come into our lives from outside to trouble us. Severe trials, great losses, and disappointed faith may make our very survival seem doubtful. But when we look to Christ who indwells us, we are sufficient for all these things.

A totally different sort of hard time, however, can arise from within us. For many reasons we can become deeply dissatisfied with ourselves. Maybe we abuse our children or fail them in other ways. Perhaps we get caught in criminal behavior. Or we become involved in personal scandal. Maybe, like Peter, we pledge that we will follow Christ anywhere but then fail or dishonor him.

Not only did Peter know what that was like, but it appears from Romans 7 that Paul did, too. He wrote, "I have the desire to do what is good, but I cannot carry it out. For what I do is not the good I want to do; no, the evil I do not want to do—this I keep on doing. . . . What a wretched man I am! Who will rescue me from this body of death?" (Romans 7:18, 19, 24).

Isaiah also stands out as one who knew the agonies of self-reproach. On one occasion he said, "Woe to me! I am ruined! For I am a man of unclean lips, and I live among a people of unclean lips, and my eyes have seen the King, the LORD Almighty" (Isaiah 6:5).

If you have ever felt miserable, worthless, and wretched because you somehow let down God, you know what a crushing experience it is. Yet the very persons we have observed as scriptural examples of self-loathing ought to encourage us. Who were these people who felt so worthless before God? Peter, Paul, Isaiah—hardly a list of losers. These are among the noblest names in all of history.

The miserable failures of these saints could very well have had much to do with their subsequent godly lives. By nature we are all flawed, fallen creatures, and until we're convinced of that at a gut level, we are ill-prepared to serve God. We tend to trust our own strength, not his, and to usurp the glory that belongs to him alone.

One would think that every Christian would know better—would understand his own inadequacy. We all come to Christ initially as sinners, totally dependent on the mercy of God for salvation. Nevertheless, we often drift back into the illusion that we are pretty good people.

The evidence that we are living in illusion comes when we fail the Lord *and then are surprised*. Why are we surprised? Didn't we originally sign on as sinners?

While a clear grasp of our own sinful inadequacy is necessary to spiritual maturity and usefulness, that is by no means the whole picture. God's dealing with his people never stops at the point of self-reproach.

The Worst of Sinners

Let's consider more closely the story of one man who failed God. Saul of Tarsus was a man of strong convictions

—and proud of it. Others *said* they believed, but he put shoe leather to it. Saul served the God of his fathers with great zeal.

There was the case of the "Way" sect, for example. Troublesome bunch, and persistent. Their leader had been put to death almost two years before. More recently, Saul helped organize the execution of Stephen, a spokesman for the cult. What a firebrand that man was! Tragic that he was caught up in error; he could have been such a force for God with all that zeal and conviction. Indeed, Stephen was not unlike Saul himself in that regard.

Such a destructive heresy as the "Way" had to be stopped. Saul owed that much to other promising young men like Stephen who might be sucked into this thing. And he owed it to God.

It was fortunate that the people were beginning to understand and to help obliterate the "Way." The effort to free Jerusalem of their presence had been almost totally successful. Damascus still had a nest of the cultists, though, and Saul must deal with them next.

He set out for Damascus armed with authority to arrest any "Way" adherents he might find. But between Jerusalem and Damascus, something happened to Saul. He was struck blind by a bright light, and at the same time thrown into stark confusion by a voice from heaven claiming to be Jesus, the executed leader of the "Way."

Blind and dazed, Saul spent the next three days doing some heavy thinking. Only God could speak from heaven like that, but the voice had identified itself as Jesus. Could Jesus really be God? Had Saul been fighting against God at the very time he was trying hardest to serve him? The possibilities were incredible and frightening.

Saul was still sightless, still without food, still struggling with the implications of everything that had happened to him when a visitor arrived. Ananias said Jesus had sent him—and incredibly, he knew all about Saul's odd experience on the road.

It was the final confirmation of what Saul now knew in his heart. Jesus was Messiah. The "Way" was God's way. And he, Saul, had done everything in his power to destroy the work of God.

Can you imagine what that knowledge did to a man proud of his service to God? To miss that far! To fail God so miserably! To have killed God's witnesses!

Ananias assured Saul that God would both forgive and use him. Saul immediately regained his sight, was baptized, and began to preach Christ. But he never forgot the sense of shame he felt over the abysmal way he had sinned against God. Almost twenty-five years later he told the Corinthian believers, "I am the least of the apostles and do not even deserve to be called an apostle, because I persecuted the church of God" (1 Corinthians 15:9).

Thirty years after his conversion, at the twilight of his life, he told Timothy that "Christ Jesus came into the world to save sinners—of whom I am the worst" (1 Timothy 1:15).

Self-Hate Can Kill

Seeing yourself as the worst of sinners can be fatal. More than one person, unable to cope with a sense of utter failure and worthlessness, has acted as his own judge, jury, and executioner. Others, like Betty Hunt, have killed themselves gradually with alcohol or drugs.

In *A True View of You*[1] I tell the true story of a ten-year-old boy who was so often and so strongly condemned by his mother that he hanged himself. His older sister had tried to intervene. Just before the hanging, she had told him, "It doesn't matter what she says, Rob. You're not that bad."

"Yes, I am," he said. "She's right. I'm no good. I can't do anything right. I shouldn't even be living."

Later that same day his sister found Rob hanging in a tree near their home and just managed to save his life.

Do you feel like such a failure before God that you shouldn't even be living? If so, you are overreacting. To see your own sinfulness and failure is okay. As we've said, many great Bible saints had that experience. If that's what is happening to you, congratulations! You finally see yourself as you are, with no flattering delusions.

But don't kill yourself. There is something else crucial for you to consider besides your own unworthiness. As Paul—the former "worst of sinners" Saul of Tarsus—put it, "Christ Jesus came into the world to save sinners" (1 Timothy 1:15). Or as Jesus himself said, "God did not send his Son into the world to condemn the world, but to save the world through him. Whoever believes in him is not condemned, but whoever does not believe stands condemned already" (John 3:17-18).

When you see yourself as unfit to live, you are right in one sense. But you must also see God as he is. He delights in mercy, forgiveness, new hope. "'As surely as I live,' declares the Sovereign LORD, 'I take no pleasure in the death of the wicked, but rather that they turn from their ways and live'" (Ezekiel 33:11).

The fact that you are alive means that in God's view you ought to be alive, for he could end your life at any time of his choice.

Each of us may view himself or herself in one of three ways. First, we may accept ourselves on the assumption that we are acceptable. By whatever standards we apply—with or without reference to God—we judge that we are okay, or at least fit to live. That was how Saul saw himself until his abrupt awakening. By contrast, Betty Hunt never did see herself that way.

Second, we may reject ourselves and judge that we are worthless as Betty and Rob did. But who can live with that?

Third, we may say, "I am a washout, a failure in myself, but God in his great mercy and love has forgiven me and will make something worthwhile out of me yet."

It is this third view that transformed Saul the persecutor into Paul the apostle. It is this view that changed Betty Hunt from promiscuous drunk to responsible and loving mother. It is this view that has worked a similar transformation in millions of others.

They were unprofitable, but became profitable. They were a liability to their world, but became an asset. They were a curse, but became a blessing. They were unfit to live, but became fit to live with God forever.

NOTES

1. Stanley C. Baldwin, *A True View of You* (Ventura, Calif.: Regal Books, 1982), pp. 79-81.

3
When Forgiveness Seems Far Away

The End of the Conflict

We haven't quite told the story about Paul and his struggle with a sense of sinful worthlessness. The problem was not resolved for all time when he came to know Christ. Maybe it should have been, but it wasn't.

So far as we know, Paul never doubted that God had forgiven him for his career as a persecutor of the church. He didn't go around being tormented about what he had done "before Christ," although he did recall those days with shame. Paul did almost self-destruct over another issue, however. He grew to hate himself for his sorry performance as a Christian.

Paul never reveals the details, but the sin that got to him was covetousness. Was it for money he lusted? For the good life he saw others enjoying? For ease? For prestige? For power? For reputation among the believers?

Maybe it was all of these, for he wrote, "But sin . . . produced in me every kind of covetous desire" (Romans 7:8).

To see this rampant in himself was a crushing experience for Paul. Even in his pre-Christian days he would have disdained such sin. He had been "in regard to the law, a Pharisee . . . as for legalistic righteousness, faultless" (Philippians 3:5-6)

When he came to know Christ, his righteousness became an inner matter of the heart instead of mere outward conformity to law. Therefore, Paul expected that he would be more righteous than before, certainly not less. Now he found the crude and vulgar sin of covetousness not only present in his life, but irresistible.

It threw him into a second crisis of self-hate. "What a wretched man I am!" he cried (Romans 7:24).

Facing Hard Facts

We think it shocking when someone who claims to be a Christian behaves reprehensibly. We wonder whether such a person is truly born again. We think that if the person is a true Christian, he or she is certainly not a very good one. Sometimes we ourselves are the "someone" who sins, and we are shocked at the shattered image of our presumed godliness.

That's hard to face.

Paul faced it and drew a conclusion from it. He didn't decide that Christ was no Savior after all. He didn't dismiss as invalid his own conversion experience. Far from it. He declared. "If I do what I do not want to do, it is no longer I who do it, but it is sin living in me that does it. . . . in my inner being I delight in God's law" (Romans 7:20, 22).

Paul exonerated himself. Or rather, he came to understand that he had been exonerated. Completely.

The bottom line for Paul was not self-hate. It was not, "Oh, how holy God is and how rotten I am!" Instead, it was "There is now no condemnation for those who are in Christ Jesus," and nothing "in all creation will be able to separate us from the love of God that is in Christ Jesus our Lord" (Romans 8:1, 39).

Nothing can separate us. It is true that great psychological and emotional forces will continue to create barriers and even conflict between us and God. But Scripture likens the believer's union with the Lord to the marriage bond that makes "one flesh" out of two people. We read, "But he who unites himself with the Lord is one with him in spirit" (1 Corinthians 6:17). That is why we should not accept the thinking of those who set forth self-loathing as a standard for Christians—essentially they tear apart what God has joined together.

Let me explain what I mean.

God As Intimidator

One writer[1] who cites Isaiah's "woe-is-me" speech (chapter 2) says, "We ought to be shaken to our roots when we see ourselves in comparison to him. If we are not deeply pained about our sin, we do not understand God's holiness." A bit later, he says, "And our sense of sinfulness and fear is proportional to our experience of the presence of God."

This would all be well and good if it were portrayed as an abiding insight or an experience preparatory to salvation. But to hold up the experience as normative Christianity is neither edifying nor true. The implication is that the more we know God, the worse we should feel about ourselves.

But that is not what the record shows. God did not leave Isaiah to wallow in his self-reproach in a "sense of sinfulness and fear." Rather, God cleansed Isaiah and then appointed him to service (see Isaiah 6:6-9). To stop at the point of self-reproach is to abort the work of God in our lives.

To carry on in this writer's line of thought tends to produce other wrong concepts also. "God punishes sin, even in those who are redeemed," the author says. It's true that God does chasten his own, as Hebrews 12:5-12 makes clear: "God disciplines us for our good, that we may share in his holiness" (v. 10). But God does not punish his own people by taking vengeance or retribution. Jesus already bore the penalty when he took on himself the punishment that we deserved for our sin.

There is a vast difference between punishing and correcting, between repaying a wrongdoer and retraining him.

I wish this were as far as the author had gone; but he went even further. He writes, "Jesus' very presence was intimidating." Several examples purport to show that Jesus terrified people. The woman who was healed by touching Jesus' garment afterward fell down before him "trembling with fear" (Mark 5:33). The writer says, "The word *trembling* is the word used in the Septuagint to describe the shaking of Mt. Sinai when God gave the law. She really shook! She was terrified. A sinner in the presence of the Holy God should be."

Pardon me?

To take this position makes Jesus a minister of Law. It ignores what Jesus said to this woman who came to him trembling. He said, "Go in peace and be freed from your suffering" (v. 34). That doesn't sound intimidating to me.

Another example cited is Peter, who at the very beginning of his association with Jesus was overwhelmed by the large catch of fish he took at Jesus' bidding. Peter said, "Go away from me, Lord; I am a sinful man!" (Luke 5:8). The writer comments "All he could see was his own sinfulness when confronted with the power and presence of Holy God. The true worshipper comes in that spirit. He is broken over his sinfulness."

But what did Jesus say to Peter in this circumstance? "Don't be afraid; from now on you will catch men" (v. 10).

To portray Jesus as Holy God who intimidates sinful

man is to risk obscuring the whole point of the gospel. Jesus came to mediate between Holy God and sinful man; to reconcile, not to intimidate.

I have no question that the writer's purpose is worthy and his concern is genuine. Like the rest of us, he wants all believers to develop a sense of reverence and awe for the Lord. And that Lord *is* holy!

But we fall into an error that is, alas, only too common. We imagine that the way to glorify God is to abase man. We think God's glory requires man's humiliation. The same writer paraphrases our Lord's "blessed are the poor in spirit" with the demeaning "blessed are the nobodies."

Is our God the God of the nobodies? Does that glorify him? Or would he receive more glory to be God of the somebodies? We read in Hebrews that when it comes to people of faith, "God is not ashamed to be called their God" (11:16). He doesn't view us as nobodies!

It's really quite the opposite. We read that God has a rich and glorious inheritance in the saints (not *for* the saints, though that's also true, but God sees us as his rich and glorious inheritance—see Ephesians 1:18). Jude tells us we are to be presented "before his glorious presence without fault and with great joy" (v. 24). We will be honored in the court of Almighty God.

We aren't nobodies. And God's glory doesn't need our self-loathing.

Whenever I encounter these how-vile-before-God-we-miserable-sinners-are teachings, my heart cries out, *Hey, haven't you heard? The war is over! God and his people have been reconciled. We aren't at loggerheads with God any more. We are not at odds. We are on the same side!*

Scripture states it even more strongly: "He who unites himself with the Lord is one with him in spirit" (1 Corinthians 6:17).

Was Jesus Wrong about the Prodigal?

To tell God's people that they always need to feel rotten about their sins is foreign to the spirit of the gospel, as portrayed in Jesus' story of the prodigal son (see Luke 15). As soon as that boy reached home, he was fully accepted and made the honored guest at a celebration.

The father didn't say, "Now, listen! I hope you realize how unworthy of forgiveness you are. You had better watch your step in the future if you expect to stay around here."

That father did not intimidate his boy; he loved him.

A sense of shame and failure may have been useful at one point if it helped bring the boy home. Perhaps his shame helped him come to his senses and choose his father's house over the miserable life in the far country. Like Betty in the previous chapter, he was at the end as well as at the bottom, and he may have gone home just to survive. In any case, the father laid no guilt trip on him once he reached home.

Suppose the son had been admitted back into the home on a "trial" basis. Suppose he had been constantly reminded of his failure. That would still have constituted better treatment than he deserved.

Knowing how bad things were in the far country, he likely would have stayed and served faithfully. But he also would have suffered emotionally from the constant reminder of his second-class status.

The elder brother would no doubt have been happy, and those who have the spirit of the elder brother are with us still.

But the father didn't see things that way. In his view, he and his son were reconciled. His son was restored as a son, not a servant.

That's grace! That's the gospel! And it shouldn't be compromised in the name of worship or holiness or anything else.

Jesus taught that those who are forgiven most will love most. And forgiven means *forgiven*. It is love and grace that keep the believer true to God, not intimidation.

Be Holy Because I Am Holy

The question is raised and must be faced: But what if a person presumes on God's love and grace? What if he carelessly or willfully sins against the light he has? Can he do absolutely anything and still be held guiltless?

Whenever a question like that arises in Scripture, words of warning follow. "As obedient children, do not conform to the evil desires you had when you lived in ignorance. But just as he who called you is holy, so be holy in all you do; for it is written: 'Be holy, because I am holy.' Since you call on a Father who judges each man's work impartially, live your lives as strangers here in reverent fear" (1 Peter 1:14-17).

Many people want firm doctrinal statements that spell out clearly just what will happen under what circumstances. They think they should have a neat system that answers all questions. But God is bigger than all our systems, and so is God's truth.

The Bible's message of grace is clear. So are its warnings against sin. We don't need to pinpoint the place where one impinges on another.

What we need to remember is that, in essence, Christianity is a relationship, not a set of rules or a list of behaviors. A person knows—*you know*—whether you have turned your face or your back toward God. To use scriptural terms: You know whether you are united to the Lord in one spirit or alienated from him.

So long as you and the Lord are on the same side, living godly will be as Betty Hunt understood it from that first day—not always easy, but always something you and your Friend can handle together.

Toward Less Moral Blindness

However genuine our love and devotion to God are, we can and do still fail him. It's so easy to think otherwise, to assume that if anything were seriously amiss in our lives the Holy Spirit would surely convict us of it. But it's not quite that simple.

Let me illustrate.

It is generally known that John Newton, who gave us one of the great hymns of all times in "Amazing Grace," was once a slave trader. What many don't know is that he continued in the slave trade long after he gave his heart and life to Christ.

He didn't realize he was sinning.

Newton had been a hard-living, profane seaman when at age twenty-two he almost perished in a storm at sea. Crying aloud to God for mercy, he was converted then and there, March 10, 1748. Immediately his life changed. His swearing ceased and he became a wonder to his fellow seamen, before whom he openly read his Bible and prayed.

Before his conversion, Newton had seen enough, one would think, to make him well aware of how wrong the slave trade was. He had worked on slave ships and witnessed the inhumane conditions firsthand. He knew the males were kept in chains down in the cargo hold, while the females were abused on deck at the whim of the crew.

Newton had also learned by experience that these blacks were human beings. During one of his early misadventures, he had been thrown into an African slave compound himself. Without food and shackled by the ankles, he would have died except that the very blacks whom he had driven with whips had compassion and took care of him.

Yet neither this nor his conversion led Newton to renounce slave trading. From 1750 to 1754, he commanded a slave ship—and held Sunday services for crew and human cargo alike. Talk about screaming inconsistency!

Almost thirty years later Newton wrote that nothing could have induced him to continue in the slave trade had he known it was wrong. "Though my religious views were not very clear, my conscience was very tender and I dared not have displeased God by acting against the light of my mind."

Newton said he never suspected his acts were wrong. To us—and even to Newton himself thirty years after the fact—that's hard to understand. To Newton's credit, he later actively supported the effort to abolish the slave trade. He played a significant role in a twenty-year struggle which ended in the abolition of slavery throughout the commonwealth in 1807, the same year that Newton died.

My question is this: How could he have blindly supported and participated in the evil of slave trading for six years after his conversion? More unsettling yet: What comparable evils may exist unsuspected in our own lives?

American Atrocities: Can It Be?

M. Scott Peck in his provocative book *People of the Lie* discusses evil from the perspective of a psychiatrist and a committed Christian. The book is awesome, and its claims and implications should be widely studied.

Most of the book focuses on individual evil. But Peck also writes about what he learned as an army psychiatrist when in 1972 he chaired a committee to recommend research on the My Lai massacre. American soldiers there murdered at least 500-600 Vietnamese men, women, and children in an atrocity that most of us have been quick to forget. Peck sees not only that atrocity but also the entire American war in Vietnam as evil. He writes:

> But how could we—we Americans—be villains? The Germans and the Japanese in 1941, certainly. The Russians, yes. But

the Americans? Surely we are not a villain-
ous people. If we were villains, we must
have been unwitting ones. This I concede;
we were largely unwitting. But how does
it come about that a person or a group or
an entire nation is an unwitting villain?
This is the crucial question.

This is a crucial question for all of us. Peck answers
the question by citing laziness and narcissism as "the twin
progenitors" of evil. Regarding the Vietnam war, he says:

As a people we were too lazy to learn and
too arrogant to think we needed to learn.
We felt that whatever way we happened to
perceive things was the right way without
any further study, and that whatever we
did was the right thing to do without re-
flection. We were so wrong because we
never seriously considered that we might
not be right. With our laziness and narcissism feeding each other, we marched off to
impose our will on the Vietnamese people
by bloodshed with practically no idea of
what was involved.[2]

Not everyone will agree with Peck about the Vietnam war being an American evil, though he makes a far
stronger case than I can report here. The point is that the
question of our culpability in Vietnam needs to be asked
and answered just as slavery needed to be questioned in
Newton's time. To refuse to ask the question betrays the
narcissism—the uncritical self-admiration—that Peck laments. To ask but not to pursue the answer betrays the
laziness he cites.

Today there are many issues which raise moral questions of which we all ought to be aware. To name a few:

world hunger
waste of food and resources

environmental pollution
domestic violence
the arms race—nuclear, germ, space
    warfare
women's rights
prison reform
racial equality
genetic engineering
religious bigotry
abortion
bureaucracy
materialism
specialization
medical care
intervention in foreign affairs
drug and alcohol abuse
tobacco price supports
state-sponsored gambling

Narcissism and laziness will lead us into unintentional evil in these and other areas. Narcissism, because in uncritical self-admiration we assume our own view must be the correct one. Laziness, because we just won't put forth the effort to study, debate, and sort out the truth.

Granted, one hasn't the time to be an expert on everything; but most of us could know a lot more than we do. We can, at least, recognize the danger of error created by our lack of understanding, and thus reduce the narcissistic arrogance that gives error its strength.

The Hope for Failing God Less

Let's summarize what we've said. We began the previous chapter with the story of Betty Hunt, a women who failed God dismally. Betty's life changed when her guilty self-hate was replaced by a sense of God's forgiveness. There is grace for those who have failed, and that grace not only forgives past failure but also gives strength to do better in the future.

Next we said that we fail God even after we become Christians, but that it doesn't invalidate our spiritual experience. Our reconciliation to God is a profound reality; we are united to him in one spirit. We are on his side now, and we must stop thinking in the old adversarial mode as if God and his people were rivals.

We said, third, that grace is not a license to sin and that God calls us to holiness. We tend to suffer from moral blindness and do wrong, as John Newton did, without even suspecting it. We attributed this blindness (at least in part) to laziness and uncritical self-admiration.

These two "progenitors of evil" are not easy to overcome, but *guess who can do it.*

Not the person who has such a load of guilt and self-loathing that he groans under its sheer weight.

Not the nobody.

Not the prodigal who has come home, but still lives in shame and under suspicion.

Not the intimidated.

Not the wretch.

Ah, but the forgiven, the strong, the hopeful, God's somebodies . . . they can endure the necessary self-criticism to see their own evil, because they operate from a secure position of union with God. They can wrestle with moral dilemma and search tirelessly for truth, for they have the energy of the Holy Spirit.

For those who know they have failed God and been forgiven, there is—at last—hope!

NOTES

1. John MacArthur Jr., *The Ultimate Priority* (Chicago: Moody Press, 1983), pp. 77-86 for this and subsequent quotes.

2. M. Scott Peck, *People of the Lie* (New York: Simon and Schuster, 1983).

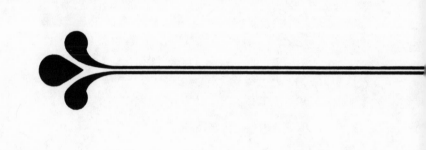

4
When You Don't Feel Spiritual

Troughs and Dark Nights

Probably every Christian of two years' standing or more knows what it is to feel unspiritual. To all of us, God sometimes seems distant. We are dry, even dusty-dry, in our souls.

More than 500 years ago, Thomas à Kempis wrote a spiritual classic, *Imitation of Christ*. He confessed, "I have found no man so religious or devout that feeleth not sometime withdrawing of grace or diminution of fervor."

Another impressive example is Brother Lawrence, the simple seventeenth-century cook from whose letters were compiled *The Practice of the Presence of God*. He seemed to be in constant fellowship with the Lord. When his times of prayer were over, he "continued with God, praising and blessing Him with all his might, so that he passed his life in continual joy." Yet even he wrote of "those times of dryness or insensibility and irksomeness in prayer, by which God tries our love to Him."

When Communion Isn't

Though one might feel unspiritual at any time, the communion service frequently makes one aware of such feelings. It's supposed to be such a sacred time—and when it isn't, we can become anxious.

Several things about communion tend to make it a spiritual peak experience. First, it focuses on the suffering our Lord Jesus Christ endured for us. The elements represent his body and blood. The accompanying words remind us that he died for us personally: "This is my body given for you" (Luke 22:19).

Second, if we come to the table properly, we have examined our hearts and lives before the Lord, confessing our sins and receiving his forgiveness.

It is hard to think of any spiritual exercises better calculated to bring us into felt communion with God. Aware of our sin and of his grace, we worship him.

Still, the communion service sometimes comes up short on the communion aspect; it decays into just another service. It becomes mechanical, like all our other "acts of worship." Like those times when we feel our prayers go bouncing off the ceiling. Like when our Bible reading degenerates into a fruitless exercise that we continue only out of a dogged sense of faithfulness—that is, if we continue it at all.

The Struggle to Sense God's Presence

I remember one communion service especially well. There was no particular reason for me to feel estranged from God. The edge was simply off my spiritual sensitivity. Our communion services were becoming routine and flat. In twenty years as pastor, I had probably administered the Lord's Supper at least 300 times.

On this occasion, I decided to bring the problem to the Lord openly, before the whole congregation at the communion service. I suspected others felt as I did, and would identify with my monologue.

Lord, sometimes I feel your presence.
Sometimes I don't, not even in church.

Sometimes I really don't; I sense your absence.

Jesus, are you here?

What about that song that describes me? The song that goes, "My heart is night, my soul is steel; I cannot see, I cannot feel . . ."

Ah, yes, Lord, I know it continues,
"For light, for life, I must appeal
In simple faith to Jesus."

But am I kidding myself when I say you are here unknown to our senses? Jesus, are you really here? I mean, it is only a song.

Wait! What was that you said when you walked the earth long ago? The line we almost always hear at prayer meeting when our numbers are small: "For where two or three come together in my name, there am I with them" (Matthew 18:20).

There am I.

Then, Lord, you really are here.

We worship you, Lord, and ask you to prepare our hearts to partake of your supper.

I don't know that we produced more sense of Christ's presence that day, but we did openly and honestly confront the problem. The response of some of the members made it clear that it was a problem they shared.

The Shame of Feeling Indifferent

It *is* a problem when our most sacred times become stale. Here we are surveying the wondrous cross on which the Prince of Glory died, and we are unmoved. If we feel anything, it is shame and consternation over our own hardness of heart. Such a condition of soul is well-depicted by the nineteenth-century poet Christina Rossetti:

Am I a stone and not a sheep
That I can stand, O Christ, beneath thy
    cross
To number, drop by drop, thy blood's
    slow loss
And yet not weep?

Not so those women loved,
Who with exceeding grief lamented thee.
Not so fallen Peter, weeping bitterly.
Not so the thief was moved.

Not so the sun and moon
Which hid their faces in a starless sky,
A horror of great darkness at broad noon.
I, only I.

Yet give not o'er
But seek thy sheep, true Shepherd of the
    flock;
Greater than Moses, turn and look once
    more.
And smite a rock.

What is the true nature of our problem when we
don't feel spiritual? And what can we do about it? Those
questions will occupy our thoughts through this chapter
and the next.

Cause One: "The Law of Undulation"
Many Causes

Spiritual doldrums such as we have been describing
do not always spring from the same cause. At least three
different phenomena, in addition to simple discouragement, can cast down our souls. This chapter considers two
causes, and the next chapter deals with the third.

One cause of unspiritual feelings relates to what C. S.
Lewis, in *The Screwtape Letters,* called "the law of undula-

tion." Human beings, he says, experience troughs and peaks in all areas of their lives. Thus he has the demon Screwtape tell his protégé Wormwood, "The dryness and dullness through which your patient is now going are not, as you fondly suppose, your workmanship; they are merely a natural phenomenon which will do you no good unless you make a good use of it."

Our times of spiritual dullness are likely to be of this sort. Certainly God could override all of this. He could manifest his presence in ways that are always sweetness and light. He could, as it were, bridge all the troughs. Indeed, it seems that he sometimes does so for new believers. But not for the long run. If he did, there would be no opportunity for our faith and faithfulness to ripen and mature.

A Time for Faith to Shine

Faith, we read, is "being sure of what we hope for and certain of what we do not see" (Hebrews 11:1). To be certain of God when we see (or feel or sense) him is easy, but faith believes in God in the absence of any such manifestations. "This is what the ancients were commended for" (v. 2).

To God, faith is as important in us as it was in the ancients. We are not only saved through faith initially, but we are to walk by faith throughout our lives. "We live by faith, not by sight" (2 Corinthians 5:7). It is in the troughs that faith has opportunity to work.

It seems odd, but it's entirely possible that God is most pleased with us when we feel least spiritual. It is then we are walking most by faith, without which it is impossible to please him.

When you don't feel spiritual, then, seize the moment. Perhaps you cannot leap to heights of spiritual joy just now, but you can plod along the paths of God by faith.

You can be a part of that great and age-long company of faithful believers of whom we read, "Therefore God is not ashamed to be called their God" (Hebrews 11:16).

Screwtape says, "[God] wants them to learn to walk and must therefore take away His hand; and if only the will to walk is really there he is pleased even with their stumbles. Do not be deceived, Wormwood. Our cause is never more in danger than when a human, no longer desiring, but still intending to do our Enemy's will, looks round upon a universe from which every trace of Him seems to have vanished, and asks why he has been forsaken, and still obeys."

Cause Two: The Dark Night of the Soul

When Darkness Closes In

A second phenomenon can make a person feel decidedly unspiritual. It is like the first, except the trough becomes a deep, unbridged chasm that threatens to swallow one completely and forever.

Catherine Spencer came to know Christ at the age of twelve and served him all her life. In her fifties she thought her battles of faith were behind her. If there was anything she was sure of, it was the rock steadfastness of her relationship with her Lord.

And then night fell.

God disappeared.

He was still *somewhere,* she had no doubt of that, but he wasn't with her.

When reading the Scripture failed to speak to her heart, Catherine thought, *Well, I didn't get anything out of that—the wrong portion, I guess. Tomorrow I'll try John.*

But though the Gospel of John had always before nurtured her soul, this time it seemed only empty words on paper. She tried to pray, but what was once sweet communion with God had become a monologue. She felt like a person locked out of her own home, knowing she had a key but frustrated over her inability to find it.

As the almost tangible void persisted, Catherine found it devastating to her relationship with other Christians. The glow on her fellow believers, especially those new in the faith, only accented the drab emptiness she felt within.

Catherine's insensitivity toward God contrasted sharply with her sensitivity toward people, especially in the innuendo of her friends. They weren't blunt about it (of course), but somehow the message came through that "You were not so good a Christian as you thought, or you wouldn't be feeling as you do now."

Catherine didn't believe that at all. She *knew* she had walked with God. The veiled accusations made her feel more alone. She began to let the phone go unanswered.

For about six months Catherine's dark night continued. Much of the time she felt like she was hanging on by her fingernails. Then one morning Catherine knelt to pray as usual and found beauty. Her communion with God was restored. She had not shed the desolation like a garment so that it would never return. But the bad times were fewer and less severe, and she knew she could manage.

In Catherine's case the dawn came slowly—but it did come, and today she is fully restored. The ordeal was still fresh in her mind when I talked with her last, and tears blurred her eyes as she described it. She had come far enough through, however, to analyze what had happened. She perceived four stages.

1. *Desperation.* She had lost contact with God, and no amount of praying, reading Scripture, or listening to Christian teaching helped in the slightest.

2. *Defiance.* She decided that if she had to walk by faith without any sense of communion with God, she would do that. "Who needs it?" she told herself. "I'll just keep on keeping on."

3. *Desolation*. She plunged into a black hole. She was like a child needing to hold on to her father's hand—but she was all alone. Already it seemed she had spent an eternity in this living hell, and for all she knew it might continue as long as she lived.

4. *Hope*. She began to see tiny glimpses of light, small as pinpricks. One day while walking down the aisle of a hospital, she overheard a snatch of conversation from a stranger. What the woman was talking about, Catherine never knew, but the words "It's true," pierced her heart. "Oh, Lord," she cried from the depths of her being, "I know it's true. I don't know what happened to it, but I know it's true."

Shortly after that episode, her communion with God was reborn. Dark times still creep in, "but those times are shorter now and not so deep," she said, a smile glistening through her tears.

I knew she would be all right.

Why Does the Dark Night Come?

I suspect that inexplicable dark nights of the soul like Catherine's are uncommon. They are far from unknown, however, and should not be dismissed lightly.

The expression "dark night of the soul" originated, as far as anyone can tell, with the sixteenth-century Spanish mystic named St. John of the Cross (who wrote a book by that title). The phrase was later borrowed by Georgia Harkness for her own book, published in 1945. Her book describes dark-night experiences of believers of all ages, including George Fox, John Bunyan, and Madame Guyon.

Harkness linked the dark night to depression, perfectionism, and other emotional ills. She suggested it involves both sin and illness, even though it usually afflicts "better" Christians. She did not think it sent arbitrarily by

God to refine the soul, though he certainly might use it to that end.

In contrast to Harkness, St. John of the Cross insisted that the dark night was to be distinguished from distress caused by sin or emotional disorders. He held that to imply that those in the dark night are suffering from "melancholy or some other imperfection with respect to sense or to spirit" is to play Job's comforters and accuse the innocent.

Maybe it can work either way. Maybe the dark night can result from emotional and spiritual problems or can come without regard to either.

Is It Depression by Another Name?

Don Baker in his book *Depression* describes his own feelings of separation from God in terms that sound like a dark-night experience.

> For hours each day I would ponder such questions as:
>
> Where is God?
>
> Why doesn't he answer me?
>
> Has God really deserted me?
>
> My theology rejected the last possibility, but my life seemingly had nothing to show for his abiding presence.
>
> My Bible kept saying to me that God is a changeless God, and yet it seemed that without explanation he suddenly had become terribly indifferent.
>
> This God of mine, who had promised never to leave or forsake, appeared now to be playing some cruel form of hide and seek. No matter how diligently I sought him, he was nowhere to be found.
>
> This God whom I had loved and served

had promised to keep his ears open to my
cries. When I prayed, however, it seemed
that he had now become stone deaf.

My Bible, always a source of strength,
had little to say to me. When it did speak,
the words were soon lost in the pall of
gloom and forgetfulness that had settled
down over my mind.

Time and again I would leaf through its
pages, seeking a promise or an explanation, only to close its covers in disappointment.[1]

Baker at length discovered that he was hypo-
glycemic, and he attributed some of his difficulties to that.
He also writes of demonic influence and of being ambiti-
ous beyond his abilities, suggesting a complex mix of factors for his depression.

By contrast, Catherine Spencer (and St. John of the
Cross) seemed to experience the dark night apart from any
discernible cause. Individual cases apparently can arise
from wholly different causes.

What Does the Bible Say?

The Scriptures never talk about a dark night of the
soul by that term. No character in Scripture serves as a
clear example of such, though Job, Jeremiah, and even
David are possible cases.

But one unique psalm, the eighty-eighth, does paint
a picture of the soul's dark night. Alexander MacLaren
says it "stands alone in the psalter, which would be incom-
plete as a mirror of phases of devout experience unless it
had one psalm expressing trust which has ceased to ask or
hope . . . but still clasps God's hand even in the 'darkness.'"

The unique thing about the psalm is not that the

writer feels deep anguish. It is not that God fails to answer his prayer. It is that he cannot get through to God at all. "But I cry to you for help, O LORD; in the morning my prayer comes before you. Why, O LORD, do you reject me and hide your face from me?" (vv. 13-14). The psalm ends in unrelieved despair. "The darkness is my closest friend."

Let There Be Light

So, then . . . what else is there to say? Our attempt to understand the dark night of the soul remains ill-defined, like the experience itself. But that does not mean there is nothing to be done, or that there is no hope. Far from it.

The first thing to do is to repent of all known sin. Certainly it is cruel and unfair for someone else to say or imply that your problem is unconfessed sin; but you do need to face that possibility. Sin *does* separate people from God. "Surely the arm of the LORD is not too short to save, nor his ear too dull to hear. But your iniquities have separated you from your God; your sins have hidden his face from you, so that he will not hear" (Isaiah 59:1-2).

A second thing to do is to get a thorough physical checkup. Don't settle for a cursory examination. Tell your doctor about the depression or darkness you are experiencing. Ask him to eliminate all possible physical causes. Don't be afraid to specify that you want a blood sugar test for hypoglycemia, and adrenal and thyroid tests. These days it is appropriate for patients to "take an interest" in their own case. If your doctor resents it or is uncooperative, perhaps you should see a different doctor.

In addition to the above-mentioned tests, if you are a young adult, you should be checked for mononucleosis. If you are a woman in menopause, you should be checked for hormonal imbalance.

A third place to seek remedy for spiritual darkness is counseling. If your own pastor or church counselor doesn't suit you, inquire about other resources in your area. Call local mental health agencies, check the yellow pages, ask recommendations of your friends. Larger cities and many mid-sized ones have Christian counseling centers, some of which base their rates on ability to pay.

Fourth, take good care of yourself. Get plenty of rest and exercise. Eat properly and use vitamins judiciously. Keep busy with constructive activities, giving yourself something else to think about besides your condition.

Fifth, keep hanging on to God. Trust his sovereignty and his love. Remember that you are indwelt by Jesus Christ. I know this will seem hard to do. "Where is God?" you may still ask. "Why this darkness? Will there ever be light again?"

Come back with me to the opening words of the Bible. "In the beginning God created the heavens and the earth. Now the earth was formless and empty, darkness was over the surface of the deep" (Genesis 1:1-2). Does that also sound like a description of your soul?

Then read on. "And the Spirit of God was hovering over the waters. And God said, 'Let there be light,' and there was light" (vv. 2-3).

I say it again. Keep hanging on to God. He raises the dead and calls into being that which was not. He once brooded over a whole world shrouded in darkness and then declared, "Let there be light," and there was light.

Your day, too, will dawn.

NOTES

1. Don Baker, *Depression: Finding Hope and Meaning in Life's Darkest Shadow* (Portland, Oregon: Multnomah Press, 1983), pp. 65, 66.

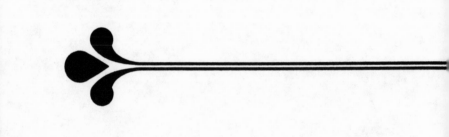

5
When Comfort Is Worse Than Pain

The Problem of Painlessness

Much has been written in recent times about *The Problem of Pain,* as C. S. Lewis called his book on suffering. *Where Is God When It Hurts?* is Philip Yancey's book on the same subject.

These are good books and they address a difficult theological and personal question: Why does a God of love permit suffering?

When we ask ourselves why we sometimes don't feel spiritual, we are confronting an issue intrinsically related to suffering.

A basic concept we need to grasp is this: *As bad as pain can be, painlessness is worse.*

This is true in a cosmic sense—God chose to make man even though he knew man would fall. Our Lord chose to experience the pain of man's fall and redemption over the painlessness of a universe without man.

True to his Father's principles, Jesus chose the pain of the incarnation and the cross over the painlessness of staying in glory and forgetting about humanity.

We sometimes make an opposite choice. We take the painless way. We choose the comfortable over the challenging, the easy over the meaningful, the safe over the rewarding. And each time we make a wrong choice of this kind, we forfeit a chunk of life.

After a few crucial bad decisions or a long list of smaller ones, we begin to wonder where our vitality went. Why are our prayers listless, our devotions routine, our entire lives boring? "Where is God when it hurts" is not our anguished question at those times. We've successfully dodged life's hurts. Our heart-cry—somewhere deep down under layers of indifference—is, "Where is God when it *doesn't* hurt?"

Who Needs Pain?

We have said that choosing painlessness leads to spiritual boredom. Does that mean we should seek to suffer in order to be fully alive to God? No. But neither should the desire to avoid pain deter us from doing the will of God when it involves suffering . . . *as it will*.

Some are vocal in teaching a contrary concept. Jesus said he came that we might have life abundantly (see John 10:10). Some interpret "abundant" to mean "painless." We should be prospering materially, physically, and spiritually, they say, not hurting in any of these areas.

Scripture Misused

One passage used to support this view is 3 John 2: "Beloved, I wish above all things that thou mayest prosper and be in health, even as thy soul prospereth" (KJV).

Please don't be offended if you have understood this to be God's message to you; but let me remind you of the important principles of Bible interpretation we stated previously (chapter 1). Not every statement in the Bible is a direct or even an indirect promise to us personally. We need to ask at least two questions about a passage in question:

1. Is this a message from God to Christians generally?

2. Does the suggested interpretation square with the rest of the Bible?

First, our passage from 3 John 2 is clearly a personal message from one friend to another—"the elder, to my dear friend Gaius" (v. 1). It is essentially a warm greeting and an expression of good will. The *New International Version* renders it, "Dear friend, I pray that you may enjoy good health and that all may go well with you, even as your soul is getting along well."

At the end of this brief letter, John writes, "I hope to see you soon, and we will talk face to face" (v. 14). Should we use that verse to teach that people should expect God will soon appear to them personally? Should they claim that "promise" and try by faith to make it a reality?

Hardly. Neither the opening greeting nor the farewell constitutes a promise from God to his people.

Second, although one could argue that the Bible envisions believers becoming prosperous in every area of life (with passages such as Joshua 1:8, Psalm 1, and John 10:10), there are other passages which must modify that concept.

"In this world you will have trouble," Jesus promised (John 16:33). "Has not God chosen those who are poor in the eyes of the world to be rich in faith?" asks James (James 2:5). "I know your afflictions and your poverty—yet you are rich! . . . Do not be afraid of what you are about to suffer," the Lord told the church at Smyrna (Revelation 2:9-10).

Prosperity teachings may be fine up to a point; but they are both false and damaging when pressed so far that they imply a good Christian should enjoy a life without pain.

No Struggle, No Strength

The church at Laodicea was characterized by people who said, "I am rich; I have acquired wealth and do not need a thing" (Revelation 3:17). Not coincidentally, God said they were "neither cold nor hot. I wish you were either one or the other! So, because you are lukewarm—neither hot nor cold—I am about to spit you out of my mouth" (vv. 15-16).

They had no pain. They were also spiritually blasé.

Dr. C.I. Scofield said years ago in another context, "Of all the needy classes of people, the neediest of this earth are not those who are having a heartbreaking, agonizing struggle for victory, but those who are having no struggle at all, and no victory, and who do not know it, and who are satisfied and jogging along in a pitiable absence of almost all the possessions that belong to them in Christ."

Note it—one can be satisfied spiritually and yet be pitiable. God has something better in mind for us than a painless, empty Nirvana. He wants us to know the incredible excitement of sharing in the life of God as his friend.

Friendship with God Means Sharing His Suffering

To say you don't feel spiritual can be another way of saying that your friendship with the Lord is not what it once was. You and he have taken divergent paths.

It's hard to maintain any friendship when paths diverge. My best friend in high school (and afterward) was Bill Smith. We spent many hours together and confided in one another. I was best man at his wedding and he was best man at mine.

Then I went into Bible college and Bill went into business. I began to think he wasn't very spiritual, and I suppose he began to think I was a fanatic. Perhaps there was some truth to both.

In any case, our personal interests diverged and our friendship cooled. We located in different cities and lost touch. Years later, residing near each other and of like mind again, we renewed our friendship. Today it's a source of satisfaction to both of us.

Friendship with God doesn't depend on geography, since he dwells everywhere. But it does depend on mutual interest and concerns. Bob Pierce, founder of World Vision, caught the spirit of friendship with God when he said, "Let my heart be broken with the things that break the heart of God." If you don't care about God's concerns, you should not be surprised that you feel unspiritual.

The Man Called God's Friend

One man in history was especially known as the friend of God. "'Abraham believed God, and it was credited to him as righteousness' and he was called God's friend" (James 2:23, see also 2 Chronicles 20:7 and Isaiah 41:8).

Being God's friend did not mean Abraham would spend his life being lulled to sleep by soft music and gentle breezes. It meant he shared God's willingness to endure pain for a purpose.

Abraham began his friendship with God by leaving his home and kindred for a promised inheritance that was miles away and years distant. He gave up the comforts of the city to spend his life in tents. He later experienced the pain of wanting but not having a son, then of sending away a son born of Hagar, then of offering up the long-awaited son of promise on Mt. Moriah . . . and much more.

Suppose that after Abraham came to know God, he had decided deep inside that he didn't want all this pain. Suppose he had settled permanently in Haran or had moved back to Ur. Would he have become known as the friend of God? I doubt it. And I doubt he would have felt spiritual, even if he had led an exemplary life as a man of God in Ur. He'd have known the problem of painlessness, the lack of an exciting presence of God in his life. He and God would have been of divergent minds, and not friends.

So if you wonder where God is, don't think the question of spirituality is settled by how you rate on some chart of dos and don'ts. The question is, have you obeyed God's call to a life of faith and purpose, even though that involves pain?

Being a Friend of Jesus

Jesus once said to His disciples, "I no longer call you servants, because a servant does not know his master's business. Instead, I have called you friends, for everything that I learned from my Father I have made known to you" (John 15:15).

One basic thing Jesus learned from his Father was this principle of *no gain without pain*. He taught his disciples about it this way: "Unless a kernel of wheat falls to the ground and dies, it remains only a single seed. But if it dies, it produces many seeds" (John 12:24).

Immediately after calling them friends, Jesus told his disciples that "You did not choose me, but I chose you to go and bear fruit—fruit that will last" (John 15:16). God's priority for us is that we be fruitful, not comfortable. When we choose to the contrary, we diverge from God's plan, our friendship with the Lord suffers, and we don't feel spiritual because we aren't.

The Pain We Don't Need

There are, of course, distortions of the principle we've been describing. One distortion is to establish a sort of misery test for Christianity. The notion is that if dodging pain leads to an unspiritual life, then the more we suffer the more spiritual we must be. The next step beyond that is to let our suffering be known so people will realize how spiritual we are.

Jesus said the hypocrites of his day looked somber and "they disfigure their faces to show men they are fasting" (Matthew 6:16). In our day we sometimes encounter sad-faced "Christians" who display their pain like a badge of righteousness and who look like they were baptized in pickle juice.

One thing the Christian community doesn't need more of is this pain-loving martyr type. When even a few of us take that route, it is too many. We not only experience pain, but we are a pain. Self-righteous people are always obnoxious to God and man alike.

Another distortion is represented by the pain-seeking emotional disorder called *masochism,* which is defined broadly as "any pleasure obtained from being abused or dominated." This also is definitely not pain of a godly sort.

To distinguish constructive pain from the destructive is not difficult. The pain we are called upon to suffer for God is always incidental. It is never our focus and never an end in itself. We don't seek it. All we seek is to live productive and faithful lives. The pain is simply there.

Must We Suffer Forever?

Though painlessness may be linked to spiritual dullness in this life, it does not follow that we must suffer forever in order to be fully alive forever.

Scripture describes the New Jerusalem like this: "Now the dwelling of God is with men, and he will live with them. They will be his people, and God himself will be with them and be their God. He will wipe every tear from their eyes. There will be no more death or mourning or crying or pain, for the old order of things has passed away" (Revelation 21:3-4).

Notice that "the old order" is to disappear. What the

new order will be, we perceive only dimly. But it will not, we are told, include pain. Of course, even this statement strongly implies that pain is a normative element of the present order.

The situation seems to be this: Being a friend of God includes accepting pain now, as he does. In the new order, there will be no pain at all. Rather, "God himself will be with them and be their God." It is God's presence that makes life vital. In this life that involves pain, but hereafter it will not.

Increasing Our Tolerance for Pain

When we speak of the problem of painlessness, we aren't saying that you ought to plan on a life of agony. Pain doesn't have to be that bad.

How much will it hurt? Sometimes more and sometimes less, but always it will be abundantly worthwhile. "Even if you should suffer for what is right, you are blessed," said Peter (1 Peter 3:14). "I consider that our present sufferings are not worth comparing with the glory that will be revealed in us," said Paul (Romans 8:18).

You can also increase your tolerance for pain. When I was a boy, I was scared to death of needles. The announcement of an inoculation program at school filled me with dread. And when the shot came, the pain seemed just as bad as I had feared it would be.

At age twenty-four I came down with acute hepatitis and spent twelve days in a hospital getting acquainted with needles. There were needles for blood tests, needles for shots, needles for intravenous feeding. I soon learned to take them in stride. They still caused me pain, and sometimes sharp pain, but they were necessary to make me better.

If I have to endure some pain to do the will of God, I should be able to accept that also, knowing that God knows what he is doing and intends to make me better.

What Kind of Pain?

In fully doing the will of God, we encounter pain as understood in its broadest sense, not just physical discomfort. Have you ever heard of a skilled craftsman or artist taking pains to do a good job? That is one kind of pain that should mark our lives as children of God.

Another type of pain we need to accept is that of exercising the discipline required to live to God's glory. It sometimes hurts to make ourselves do what we should instead of what we want. It especially hurts when self-pity gets in and we start thinking how hard it is.

A remedy for self-pity is to think of what Christ bore on the cross for us. Our little pains of self-discipline don't seem like much by comparison. We can remember, too, that the Christ of the cross indwells us, and he hasn't changed. He is still willing to endure the cross for the joy to follow. We are not going to feel very spiritual if we silence the spirit of Christ in our hearts in order to choose comfort.

The Pain of Shyness

Yet a third type of pain involves relating to people for Jesus' sake. Have you ever heard of a person being painfully shy? In following God fully, such a person will endure the pain required to mix with other people.

Harry Bose immediately comes to mind as a classic example of someone painfully shy. He could hardly speak to another person in a social situation. His face turned red, he shifted his weight from one foot to the other, and when he finally spoke his voice came from way down in his throat so that you could hardly hear him.

Harry was a big, strong farmer, about thirty-five years old when I first met him. He was a bachelor, of course, since he couldn't talk to a man, much less a woman.

Harry's friend, Lloyd Porter, was just the opposite—an outgoing, fun-loving guy who seemed comfortable with everybody. Lloyd was a Christian.

It wasn't easy for Harry to accept Lloyd's invitation to come to church, involving as it did painful social contact with others. At last he came, though, and he kept on coming. Harry never did get over his shyness completely, but he did walk the aisle to receive Christ. Later he walked the aisle again when he married Sallie Hooper, whom he'd invited to church. In due time he became an elder.

In church board meetings Harry found it painful to speak up, but when he did, people listened, for he spoke with wisdom and grace. Today, more than one person has reason to be thankful that Harry did not choose the painless path.

If you follow the search for painlessness very far, you will likely end up not only out of touch with God, but out of touch with life. All will seem such a weariness.

Live, Don't Exist

Scripture says, "The widow who lives for pleasure is dead even while she lives" (1 Timothy 5:6). The principle applies equally to those who aren't widows.

Some time ago I read about a woman who seems to represent the very antithesis of being dead while she lives. *Virtue* magazine carried an interview with Ann Kiemel Anderson, who wrote a book a few years ago entitled *I'm Out to Change My World* and another called *I Love the Word Impossible*. You get the idea just from the titles that she is not a passive, bored-with-life person.

The interviewer asked Ann how she had kept her faith growing and alive over many years. She replied: "I think most people lose their enthusiasm because they lose touch with life. They don't get close to people and love them, feel with them, cry with them and hurt with them.

When you're really close to them and loving them and reaching out to them, somehow it makes Jesus so real because he's so much a part of all of that."

Not everyone is comfortable with that formulation. "I don't reach out to people in order to get close to Jesus," some say. "Rather, it's being close to Jesus that enables me to reach out to people."

If that's what is happening in your life, great. If you feel close to Jesus and as a result you are loving and serving others, you don't need any advice from me.

But I am writing to you who don't feel spiritual, and particularly to you whose doldrums trace to a Dead Sea syndrome. You have taken in and taken in, but haven't given out because of the cost, the risk, the pain.

Get close to people, love them, cry with them and hurt with them. Not only will you find Jesus is "part of all that," but you'll likely find he's freshly alive in you.

Part 2

Getting Through the Toughest Times

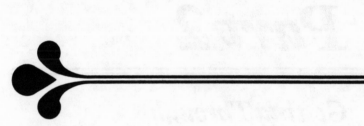

6
When You Have Every Reason to Worry

Why "Don't Worry" Is Bad Advice

WORRY: mental distress or agitation resulting from concern usually for something impending or anticipated: ANXIETY (Webster's Seventh New Collegiate Dictionary).

If you are worried about anything, you had better not show it. At least not around some of the brethren. You are likely to be whacked with a Bible passage: "Do not be anxious about anything, but in everything, by prayer and petition, with thanksgiving, present your requests to God. And the peace of God, which transcends all understanding, will guard your hearts and your minds in Christ Jesus" (Philippians 4:6-7).

"See," you are told, "the Bible says we are not to be anxious. When we are anxious, we are not trusting God. Worry is just plain sin."

Great. You have as much as ever to worry about, but now you also have a load of guilt to carry. You've just been diagnosed as living in sin.

Superficial Solutions

Most of us are adept at handling worry as long as it concerns other people's problems. Too often, like the false prophets of Jeremiah's day, we "heal the brokenness of the daughter of My people superficially, saying, 'Peace, peace,' but there is no peace" (Jeremiah 8:11 NASB).

We glibly say, "Don't worry, everything is going to be all right." Those easy words have offered but slight comfort to countless people who soon found everything was *not* going to be all right. They had every reason to worry.

A child is missing. Despite the fact that thousands of children disappear each year, never to be seen again, someone is almost certain to tell the anxious parents, "Don't worry; I'm sure you'll find her (or him) soon."

A teenager gets into trouble with the authorities. "Don't worry," a well-meaning friend tells the parents. "He (or she) will be all right. It seems they all have to sow a few wild oats." He fails to mention that some of these wild-oat sowers are only beginning a long and tragic series of wrong choices leading to misery.

A man loses his job. "Don't worry," people say. "You will find something else soon." This despite the fact that the man may be virtually unemployable because of his age and a changing job market.

Someone is sick and it's not just the flu. Doctors don't seem to know for sure what's wrong, but friends and family say, "Don't worry; you'll be all right." They say this even though some disease will sooner or later take the life of every person on earth who is not either killed or raptured.

Now, it's fine to comfort and encourage people, and I am not suggesting we predict the worst when worrisome circumstances arise: "You may never see that child again!"

No, no. But what we ought to do is speak the truth: "God cares, and God will see you through this ordeal."

What we ought not do is advocate an unworry based on a denial of reality. Sometimes people have every reason to worry, and to pretend they do not is to take residence in fantasyland.

"But if you are a Christian all things work together for good," someone says, "and everything will be all right, even if seemingly bad things happen. God's word tells us not to worry."

Still, doesn't it seem just a bit glib to dismiss worry casually? Our examples imply that the reason one shouldn't worry is that the thing feared won't happen. The fact is that the things people fear may indeed come upon them. Some certainly will.

To Worry or Not to Worry

The "mental distress for something anticipated" which the dictionary calls *worry* is actually a form of fear. Once we grasp this, we can begin to see that there is both appropriate and inappropriate worry (fear).

Some deny this. They are as critical of fear as they are of worry, and again they cite Scripture: "There is no fear in love; but perfect love casteth out fear; because fear hath torment. He that feareth is not made perfect in love" (1 John 4:18, KJV).

But we should remember what C. S. Lewis said:

> Perfect love, we know, casteth out fear. But so do several other things—ignorance, alcohol, passion, presumption, and stupidity. It is very desirable that we should all advance to that perfection of love in which we shall fear no longer, but it is very undesirable, until we have reached that stage, that we should allow any inferior agent to cast out our fear[1]

Even in this state of imperfect love, however, fear makes no sense when:

- the anticipated event is unlikely to happen
- the consequences, even if the event happens, are relatively trivial

Worry is irrational when it causes people to fret over circumstances that fall into either of these two categories. The worrier stews and fusses because this or that *might* happen—even though the chances are perhaps 1,000 to 1 against it, or it wouldn't make that much difference anyway. He or she is agitated—and probably agitates everyone else around—because it *could* happen.

Anne has a son in eighth grade at a Christian school. To get there he has to take public transportation. Anne is worried. What if her son is delayed for some reason after school and misses the bus?

Let's test Anne's worry by the standards we've suggested. First, is the anticipated event likely to happen? Anne thinks that sooner or later it is.

Second, are the consequences of missing the bus serious or trivial? Since the city buses run every twenty minutes or so all day long and far into the night, it is a trivial matter if an eighth grader misses his bus. Anne's worry is inappropriate in light of these facts.

A Time to Worry

L. E. Maxwell, the late principal of Prairie Bible Institute, once editorially "lamented and exposed the departure of a young minister from the orthodox faith." In reaction the minister threatened to sue him for libel. Maxwell describes his worry:

> I cannot tell all the misery through which I passed during the ensuing months. I would wake up in the wee hours of the morning with my mind racing like a windmill out of control. When I would try to find a sermon to preach, my mind would

be tortured with anxiety. Even while on my knees seeking God for a message, I would be torn with fear and worry about the future. I could see myself in prison with my hair shaved off and wearing striped clothes. Even when I walked downtown I fancied I saw an officer coming to arrest me.[2]

Again, let's test the worry by the standards we've established. Was the anticipated event likely to happen? Apparently Mr. Maxwell did have reason to think he was in danger of being sued for libel.

Would the consequences be serious or trivial? Exactly how serious the consequences would be is difficult to evaluate from a distance. The best guess is that the threat was not nearly so great as Mr. Maxwell imagined.

Libel suits are hard to win. The plaintiff must show first that the statements were false, second that they were made with malice or serious negligence, third that they were actually damaging. Even then the defendant would face a financial judgment rather than a prison sentence.

Nevertheless, the consequences would have been serious. Losing a libel suit would be costly in terms of money and reputation. It would dishonor the Lord and hurt the work to which Mr. Maxwell had dedicated his life. Even if he won the suit, the charges alone could do great damage.

By our tests, then, Mr. Maxwell did have reason to worry; fear about an anticipated event was legitimate.

Although he was thoroughly familiar with the biblical admonitions against worry, and although he tried to obey them, Mr. Maxwell was unable to find peace. Ultimately he stopped worrying only when he was "quite sure the case would never come up."

Five years later in an unrelated incident, Maxwell said something on a radio broadcast that a friend commented afterward was "too much." Immediately Maxwell recalled his old libel worries: "There was no mistake about it. I recognized the same issue, the same worry, the same distraction of mind. I also sensed the finger of God's just accusation."

Note the double whammy: Worry, complicated by guilt over the failure to trust God and to obey his Word that says, "Be anxious for nothing."

At last Mr. Maxwell recognized and confessed "my unwillingness to be identified with the Cross, my secret dislike to bear shame for his name, my inward refusal to rejoice in being counted worthy to suffer reproach . . . then I knew peace."

According to this testimony, then, worry was a *friend* to grace. It brought Maxwell to embrace the cross and to a spiritual growth that would not have occurred had he been able simply to dismiss all his concern and anxiety.

Had there been nothing to fear—or had he denied the threat was real—he would not have been "crowded to Christ" in repentance and renewed faith.

Sometimes It Helps to Worry

Those who say "don't worry" commonly offer plausible arguments against it. "So God can use worry to turn people to him. He can use sin and guilt that way too, but that doesn't make them desirable or right."

"Granted, bad things sometimes do happen. It certainly doesn't help to worry about them beforehand."

"Misfortunes come whether we worry about them or not. All we do when we worry is prolong the suffering. We add worry time to our hurting time."

In some cases these statements are true. The Bible certainly does not advocate a life style dominated by worry, fear, and negative thinking. Neither should we. Case studies show, however, that appropriate worry helps in the very situations in which denial is neither beneficial nor honest.

Carl was a strong man in his early forties. He had worked outdoors all his life and his body was lean and hard. He didn't drink, he didn't smoke, and he didn't worry. He was not a high risk for heart disease, but he had it nevertheless. Doctors scheduled him for heart bypass surgery.

Carl was not worried about the surgery. The doctors assured him that such an operation was, in Carl's words, "no big deal any more"—routine, really. And his overall physical condition was very much in his favor.

I visited Carl in his hospital room the night before his surgery. He was so chipper you'd have thought he was going on vacation the next day. I didn't sense it was all a brave front, either. Carl wasn't worried.

The surgery went as routinely as the doctors had predicted, and Carl's prognosis afterward was good. A couple of days later I talked with his wife. Carl wasn't doing well. He was depressed, resentful, and angry. He was in pain. And he seemed worried—about his health, about his ability ever to do his job again, about his family, about finances. Carl eventually recovered, but his convalescence was slower and more difficult than anyone had expected. I couldn't understand it.

How You React Makes a Difference

Some time later while doing research for my book *How to Build Your Christian Character,* I ran across a report that threw considerable light on the mystery of Carl's poor recovery.

In *The Quest for Self-Control,* Dr. Irving L. Janis, Yale professor of psychology, described studies of three types of patient attitudes before surgery. Patients in the first grouping were "constantly worried and agitated." Those in the second grouping were "occasionally tense or agitated." The third grouping consisted of those who were "constantly cheerful and optimistic . . . no observable agitation or tension."

The studies concluded that:

1. Persons who were *extremely fearful* before the operation were *more* likely than others to be anxiety-ridden again afterwards, and their excessive fears of body damage were linked with numerous clinical signs of chronic neurotic disturbance.

2. Persons who displayed a *moderate* degree of preoperative fear were significantly *less* likely than others to display any form of emotional disturbance during the stressful period of postoperative convalescence.

3. Persons who showed a relative *absence* of preoperative fear were *more* likely than others to display disturbed reactions of anger and intense resentment during postoperative convalescence.[3]

Carl seemed to fit very well into Dr. Janis's third category. He hadn't worried about his surgery in advance and he had paid for it afterward.

In contrast to Carl, Marge was informed by her doctor before major surgery that she would have considerable pain afterward. "The third day is usually the worst," he said.

When Marge felt rotten on the third day after surgery, she remembered the doctor's words and took courage. Though she was feeling worse, it didn't mean things were going wrong. She had no reason to panic or worry. *No doubt I will feel better tomorrow,* she thought. And she did.

According to Dr. Janis, not only surgery but any

"stressful life situation" calls for "reality-oriented" worrying. Besides surgery patients, he reported on women in labor, cancer patients, civilian air-raid victims, women whose sons and husbands were sent to war, and combat pilots. In all these situations, those who worried realistically coped with stress better than those who did not.

It was also true that those who worried excessively did worst of all in coping with difficulty when it came.

Dr. Janis writes that people reveal a "powerful, spontaneous tendency to *deny* the possibility of being personally afected by an impending source of danger." In other words, some people don't worry when they should. Let me cite the ultimate example.

When Not Worrying Brings Death

An evangelist preaches the gospel. He faithfully proclaims that Christ died for our sins, was buried, and rose again. He concludes by inviting people to receive Christ as savior, and says, "Whoever believes in the Son has eternal life, but whoever rejects the Son will not see life, for God's wrath remains on him" (John 3:36).

A man hears the message and weighs his decision. The Bible says that if he rejects Christ, God's wrath will remain on him. He thinks of the absolute horror that suggests. Just at this point an inner voice says, "Don't worry, you'll be all right."

There it is—the "powerful, spontaneous tendency to deny" the danger.

My question is this: Should the man worry?

Clearly, he should. And he should continue to worry until, by turning in faith to Jesus Christ, he deals with the danger that hangs over his head.

It sometimes *does* help to worry, and never more so than when one worries enough about his relationship to God to cry out for mercy and forgiveness.

NOTES

1. C. S. Lewis, *The World's Last Night* (New York: Harcourt, Brace & Co., copyright 1952 by C. S. Lewis), p. 109.

2. L. E. Maxwell, "Worry," *Prairie Harvester,* Spring 1983.

3. Irving L. Janis, "Psychodynamic Aspects of Stress Tolerance," in *The Quest for Self Control,* ed. Samuel Z. Klausner (New York: The Free Press, a division of the Macmillan Co., 1965), p. 226.

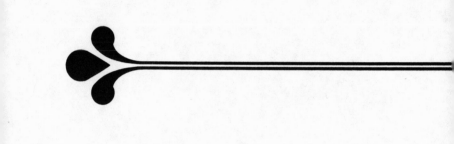

7
When Anxiety Threatens to Overwhelm You

Solving the Worry Problem

Charles Darwin knew the frustration of a worry he could not control. "I cannot enjoy the present happiness," he said, "for anticipating the future, which is about as foolish as the dog who dropped the real bone for its shadow." Even though he saw clearly the folly of his worry, he kept on worrying.

So did L. E. Maxwell, despite his knowledge of the Bible's admonitions against it.

If neither Darwin's common sense nor Maxwell's Bible knowledge solved their worry problems, what can? "The unfolding of Thy words gives light; it gives understanding to the simple" (Psalm 119:130, NASB). We need to look deeper, to really "unfold" God's word on worry.

The Worries of Paul

It is interesting that Paul, who tells us not to worry (Philippians 4:6), also seems to say in other places that he himself does worry. What can this mean?

First, it is true that concern and worry are two different things—they need to be distinguished. The dictionary says that worry is "mental distress or agitation resulting from concern . . ."

Anxiety or worry is stronger than concern. One might say that when concern takes control, it becomes worry.

In the Greek New Testament, as in English, we find two different words to describe greater and lesser degrees of care or concern. When Paul writes to "be *anxious* for nothing," he uses *merimnao*. By contrast, when he writes just a few lines further on that the Philippians have kindly renewed their *concern* for him, he uses the other word, *phroneo* (v. 10).

It all seems to work out rather neatly; we can say to go ahead and be concerned *(phroneo)*, but don't let your concern become anxiety *(merimnao)*.

Unfortunately, this neat packaging comes untied when Paul uses *merimnao* to describe Timothy's commendable anxiety over the church. "I have no man likeminded, who will naturally *care* for your state." So reads Philippians 2:20 in the King James Version. The New International Version translates it with the extremely weak phrase, "takes a genuine interest." In the original it is the strong word *merimnao*.

It's worth noting that Paul describes Timothy as being likeminded with himself in this regard. Does that mean Paul worried over the Philippian church? Not only does it sound that way here, but Paul declares as much elsewhere. "Besides everything else, I face daily the pressure of my concern *(merimna)* for all the churches" (2 Corinthians 11:28).

A Prescription, Not a Condemnation

What shall we think of this seeming contradiction in Paul? He tells the Philippians not to worry but declares that he himself does.

Various explanations have been suggested. Some say it's simply a contrast between the ideal and the real. The ideal is to have no anxiety, and we should strive for that. Nevertheless, Paul was human and he admitted that he sometimes worried.

But Paul clearly laments that the only ones who worried about the churches were himself and Timothy—hardly a proper attitude to have if his worry was a weakness (or a *sin,* as some have declared it to be).

Others seek an explanation in the differing subjects of concern. In the natural, we worry about things we perceive as threats to ourselves. Worry is self-centered. That is what Paul condemned, telling the Philippians to commit their personal concerns to God in prayer instead of worrying over them. (I'm not sure how that helps, though. Wouldn't that make our *prayers* self-centered? Is that any better?)

By contrast, Paul worried about the churches, about the spiritual welfare of others rather than his own needs.

The problem with this explanation is that Paul wrote, "Be anxious for *nothing.*" He didn't distinguish between selfish and unselfish concerns. Besides, many of the worries that most torment people today are for others: for children, for mates, for friends.

Furthermore, when we worry about others we are worrying for ourselves at the same time. We love these others for whom we are concerned, and when they hurt we hurt. That is certainly how it was with Paul and the churches (see 2 Corinthians 11:29). The distinction between selfish and unselfish worry seems dubious.

A third and better explanation is that the admonition

"be anxious for nothing" is not a condemnation of worry but a prescription for dealing with it.

Dr. Duane Dunham, Professor of New Testament Language and Exegesis at Western Conservative Baptist Seminary, says the verb here is in the present negative imperative and may be translated, "Don't go on worrying."

Paul here admonishes us to resolve our anxieties rather than retaining them. Worry should not be open-ended, a treadmill to nowhere. Indeed, that is the difference between what we might call constructive worry and neurotic worry. Neurotic worry does not lead one to emotional mastery over the perceived threat. Constructive worry does lead to such mastery. Consequently, as we saw in the previous chapter, constructive worry makes one better able to cope with stress.

Starving Birds and Stunted Lilies

Jesus' most extensive teaching on worry is found in Matthew 6:25-34. The passage is simple and yet puzzling. Taken alone, some of Jesus' statements seem to urge a life free not only of worry but of work. "Look at the birds of the air; they do not sow or reap or store away in barns, and yet your heavenly Father feeds them. Are you not much more valuable than they?" (v. 26).

Jesus sounds even more anti-work in his next example: "See how the lilies of the field grow. They do not labor or spin" (v. 28).

It's obvious that the human race could not survive if no one worked, and we have little respect for those who avoid honest labor. We might say, then, that idleness is for the birds.

But does it really serve even them? Though they do not sow seed or store the harvest, they certainly do forage for food. And they work hard to build their nests. Thus their God-given instincts help them provide for future needs, even as we human beings secure our future through forethought.

Most commentators point out that Jesus both precedes and follows his bird and flower illustrations with the admonition: "Do not worry" (vv. 25, 34). He is not teaching laziness or carelessness, they say, but trust. Work is needful—and yes, even foresight—but worry is useless.

Unfortunately, that doesn't quite explain the passage. One major problem remains. Am I not to worry because I see birds and flowers effortlessly prospering under God's care? Fine, but then what am I to do when I see birds starving in a hard winter and flowers choked out with weeds? These things do happen.

Considering the context helps. Jesus tied his worry teaching to a larger principle by beginning it with the word *therefore* (v. 25). What is the previously expressed principle upon which "don't worry" is based? "No one can serve two masters," Jesus said. "You cannot serve both God and Money" (v. 24).

The Lord continually brought people back to the basic truth that God alone must have first place in our lives. We must not be so distracted by other concerns—even for the necessities of life—that he ceases to be our focus. We need to work, to plan for the future, to be concerned about necessities. But always we need to "seek first his kingdom and his righteousness" (v. 33).

What does this passage mean? It teaches the same lesson as does the parable of the seed and the sower, that we are not to allow our hearts to become thorny ground in which the "worries of this life" choke the Word, making it unfruitful (Matthew 13:22).

Worry must never be allowed to crowd out God. But worry does not always crowd out God. It can instead crowd us to God, and that is exactly what happens when we obey the admonition, "Don't keep on worrying, but go to God in prayer" (Philippians 4:6-7).

The End of All Worry Is Not Yet

The Sermon on the Mount, of which the "don't worry" passage is a part, gives the "laws of the kingdom." Matthew's entire work represents the "Gospel of the Kingdom." Whatever your view of the Millenium, it's safe to say that the kingdom of God has not yet been fully established in the world. The meek have not inherited the earth and sin's curse has not been lifted.

Remember that before the curse, life in the Garden of Eden was much like the scene Jesus described in the passage before us. Birds did not have to scratch frantically for food. The lilies of the field did not have an uphill battle against thorns and thistles.

In Eden man lived in abundance. But when Adam sinned, God said that the earth would no longer bring forth its abundance for him as before. Instead he would eat his bread by the sweat of his face (see Genesis 3:17-19).

But back to our passage: When Jesus said not to worry about what to eat because God will provide, he was describing the conditions of the kingdom, a glorious state which has not yet fully come. It is true that sin's curse has already been mitigated, thanks to the blessings of the gospel. Thus the sheer toil required to make a living has often been reduced and the threat of starvation somewhat alleviated.

The curse, however, is still with us. Some birds perish from hunger and cold every winter. Some lilies never bloom. And some people, much more precious to God than birds or lilies, suffer and die from want.

Jesus said that the God who feeds the birds of the air and clothes the lilies of the field will do much more for us. But he still described his own as sometimes having their needs met . . . and sometimes not. Jesus said that he himself, as represented by his people, was "hungry and you gave me nothing to eat, . . . I needed clothes and you did not clothe me" (see Matthew 25:42-43).

The apostle Paul, as one who did seek first the kingdom of God, should have found "all these things"—such as food, clothing, and shelter—provided as well (Matthew 6:33). And generally they were. Yet Paul wrote, "I have known hunger and thirst and have often gone without food; I have been cold and naked" (2 Corinthians 11:27).

So what are the facts?

God is loving and kind. Usually we needn't have any worry about the essentials of life. It is not likely we'll starve. If want does threaten, however, our concern must not be allowed to come between us and our Lord.

How to Worry Well

Paul's prescription for worry is prayer. "Be anxious for nothing, but in everything by prayer and supplication with thanksgiving let your requests be made known to God. And the peace of God, which surpasses all comprehension, shall guard your hearts and your minds in Christ Jesus" (Philippians 4:6-7, NASB).

The very act of prayer, if it is genuine, has profound implications for worry. Prayer brings God into the situation. When God comes in, hopelessness goes out. Though we may be powerless to influence the course of worrisome events, God is not. He can find our lost child, correct our wayward teen, supply gainful work to the unemployed, heal the sick.

He can, but sometimes he does not.

Honesty in prayer surely recognizes that God does not always grant our petitions. We might still have reason to worry even after we've made our requests. So the Scripture goes on to say ". . . by prayer and supplication *with thanksgiving.*"

Here's the critical part: Give thanks. While praying over a concern, I cannot honestly thank God for granting my request if I don't know that he will do so. Sometimes he may give assurance that he will—and in such cases, with the answer on the way, worry evaporates. But in the absence of such assurance, I must either play mind games and try to "claim by faith" what I want, or I must acknowledge that things may not turn out my way.

If I am to thank God even if I cannot thank him for granting my petition, for what shall I give thanks? For past mercies. For his often-demonstrated love. For grace to bear hard times. For who he is.

As I pray and give thanks, my worry is resolved. Not on the basis of a fantasy that bad things won't happen, but realizing that if and when they do, God still lives and will be there with me.

It is said that Martin Luther once went through an extended period of depression and worry. One day his wife came to him dressed in mourning clothes.

"Who has died?" asked Luther.

"God," said his wife.

"God!" said Luther. "How can you say such a thing?"

"I am only saying what you are living," said his wife.

Luther realized he was living as if God were no longer alive and watching over them in love. Immediately, he changed his attitude.

That is what giving thanks will do for us; it will change our attitudes.

The Work of Worry

When real threats confront us, we should work through our worry prayerfully. Doing so includes the following steps:

1. *Face the threat.* Denying real dangers is not an act of bravery but of cowardice. It is not wisdom but folly. And it certainly is not faith; it's dishonesty.

Say, "Father, this is what I'm facing, and it has got me worried."

2. *Reassure the mind.* Though the threat is real, it is also limited. Sometimes it helps to mentally create a worst-case scenario. When you put specifics to the worst thing that could happen in your situation, things come into perspective and nameless horror and dread gives way to, "I wouldn't like it, but I could cope with it."

When you face the threat, you can be reassured with the divine promise, "As your days, so shall your strength be" (Deuteronomy 33:25, RSV). Note that this is no assurance the days won't be awesome, but rather that the grace of God will be sufficient.

Say, "Father, I thank you for putting a hedge about me and allowing Satan to proceed only so far against me. I thank you for your promise to be with me always."

3. *Plan counter-measures.* Almost always one can do something to control or reduce anticipated damages. Think about measures to mitigate pain, limit injury, neutralize opposition, increase your own strength. Approach the trial by thinking, *If such and such does happen, this is what I can and will do.* The panic and sense of helplessness that breed resentment and anger in the non-worrier will not likely overwhelm the one who has anticipated and planned ahead for the very thing that is now happening.

Say, "Thank you, Lord, for the helps that you provide. Give me wisdom and clarity of mind to make the best use of all such helps." Then ask God specifically what to do about each element of the fear you face.

When Jesus Worried

Did Jesus ever worry?

Unthinkable, someone says.

Shortly before Jesus told the disciples to consider the birds and not to worry over what to eat, he was faced with that very issue himself. He had been forty days and nights without food, alone in the wilderness. With his fast over, he needed to eat. How would he ever get back to civilization without some strengthening nourishment?

Satan suggested he turn stones into bread. It was his strategy to focus attention on Jesus' concern for his survival. More was involved than hunger pangs—Jesus had already mastered hunger in fasting for forty days. But he needed nourishment.

If Jesus did worry about what he would eat, however, he did not worry to the point of putting that concern ahead of "the kingdom of God and his righteousness." He refused Satan's suggestion, and afterward angels came and ministered to him.

Whether you believe that Jesus ever worried about food, he certainly worried about the cross. Remember Webster's definition? "Worry: mental distress or agitation resulting from concern usually for something impending or anticipated."

Words could hardly describe Jesus' travail in the Garden any better. Such was our savior's mental distress and agitation that he sweat what looked like great drops of blood while imploring the Father to spare him the impending ordeal of the cross.

But the worry and dread of the cross never came between Christ and his Father. As much as he wanted to avoid the cross, he wanted more to do the will of God. "My Father, if it is not possible for this cup to be taken away unless I drink it, may your will be done" (Matthew 26:42).

Jesus on his knees in Gethsemane is our model for dealing with worry. You and I will never face a worry more wrenching. But we may face concerns utterly devastating to us. When we do, an easy "don't worry" is not likely to help. "Don't *just* worry," is far better counsel, "but urgently take your request to God." He may grant your petition. Or he may summon you instead to a hill called Calvary. If he does, and you agree to go there because the Christ of the cross indwells you, it will be with a heart full of peace that passes understanding.

8
When You've Lost Everything

A Rickety Object Lesson

I was driving my family from Three Hills, Alberta, to Portland, Oregon—a distance of about 1,000 miles. Our car was a fourteen-year-old Dodge. Behind us we towed an even older homemade "mobile home." Dodge in those days boasted about its cars' dependability, and for good reason. My Dodge really *was* dependable.

But the trailer was something else.

It simply wasn't roadworthy. The weight was poorly balanced, and the contraption was too heavy both for the tires and for the hitch.

We spent Easter Sunday on the road with this jerry-built rig. Not that we planned it that way. We had intended to be home by Easter. But the spring breakup had left frost heaves all over what had once been a passable highway through the Canadian Rockies. We finally hit one bone-jarring pothole too many, and the steel hitch cracked.

We limped into the nearest outpost of civilization, a dingy and depressing coal-mining town. There we sat until a local garage owner took pity on us and interrupted his holiday long enough to weld our hitch.

Now, if only the tires hold, I thought as we began rolling once again. I had overinflated them to compensate for the excess load, but still they flexed alarmingly. The road was giving them a brutal pounding, too. What would I do if they failed?

"I ought to run that miserable trailer off into the ditch, take our dependable Dodge, and go on home," I said, as much to myself as to Marge. But one thing checked me. That was my frugal (it sounds better than stingy) nature. We paid good money for that trailer, and if we ever got it back to Portland we could live in it.

As I deliberated whether to leave the trailer behind (and thereby lose most of the little we possessed of material value on this earth), a spiritual truth suddenly became very clear. Whether my hitch broke or not, whether I ever got home with that trailer or not, certain secure possessions were mine. God had forgiven my sins and had given me eternal life. Everything in that trailer might perish, but not I. Not I.

A favorite psalm came to mind:

> Praise the Lord, O my soul; all my inmost being, praise his holy name. Praise the Lord, O my soul, and forget not all his benefits. He forgives all my sins (Psalm 103:1-3).

I had noticed before that the first "benefit" the psalmist praised God for in this passage was the forgiveness of sins. David rejoiced in the one asset he had that circumstances could not take away. I had that same imperishable asset.

As it turned out, we made the rest of the trip without incident (of course, the roughest part of the road was behind us). The frustration of that Easter has long since faded, but something from the experience has remained to this day. It is something that provides a wonderful support in tough times.

And what is that? When everything else seems lost, the eternal life that Jesus gives is the one irreducible asset that all believers—including you and I—can cling to.

Now, I realize that my little tale of Rocky Mountain woe might sound trivial to some beleaguered reader. No matter what became of our trailer, we still had our health, our youth, our families, our friends. We weren't even close to losing everything.

But that's typical. People often mistakenly think they have lost everything, or are about to lose everything, when it's simply not true. What has happened?

They've focused on what's lost rather than on what's left.

Some years ago I read about a seventeen-year-old boy in Waukesha, Wisconsin, who killed himself. A newspaper account said he left a note to the effect that, "without my driver's license, I don't have a car, a job, or a social life, so I might as well end it all right now."

Because he had lost his driver's license, he thought he had lost everything. And because he thought everything was lost, he killed himself. As a result, for him, everything *was* lost.

The View from Prison

The imprisoned apostle Paul celebrated what he had in Christ. He didn't focus on his lost freedom. He rejoiced in the same assets of forgiveness and eternal life that encouraged me on the dismal Easter I wrote about earlier. Because of these imperishable assets, his spirit soared even in prison.

Notice this strong theme in the beginning of his letter to the Ephesians. "Praise be to the God and Father of our Lord Jesus Christ, who has blessed us in the heavenly realms with every spiritual blessing in Christ" (Ephesians 1:3).

In "the heavenly realms"? Whatever kind of prison Paul occupied, we can be sure it was no "heavenly realm." Far from it! No, Paul was describing the dwelling places of his soul, not his physical surroundings. He was celebrating the spiritual blessings he enjoyed despite his imprisonment.

As the apostle continued writing, he repeatedly broke into praise for the grace of God. His enthusiasm tumbled out in joyful phrases piled one on top of another. If you have trouble understanding the first chapter of Ephesians, that might be why. One of the important things we teach writers is to make sentences short and simple. Paul forgot all about that as he celebrated his blessings in Christ.

Perhaps it was *because* Paul was in prison that he had time to meditate on the blessings of God until his heart overflowed in this letter of praise. Just so, tough times may prompt us to examine our own lives. They may bring us up short, make us do some heavy thinking. Do we really have any imperishable assets, or not? If so, what are they?

In pondering those questions as they apply to your life, it might help to notice the blessings Paul identified in Ephesians 1 as part of his spiritual inheritance as a Christian.

Chosen, Not Targeted

The first blessing Paul cites is that he was *chosen*. "He chose us in him before the creation of the world" (v. 4). It meant a great deal to Paul that God, before he ever made the earth, looked down through time and chose him. Perhaps the best way to understand how much it meant is to consider the opposite—what it can mean not to be chosen.

It's the feeling you have as a child when your classmates choose up sides to play ball, and you don't happen to play well. The captains start selecting their team members, and of course they choose the best players first. And there you wait suffering. Joe is chosen and Bill is chosen and Bob is chosen, and they go stand beside their captains. The group of not-yet-chosens gets smaller and smaller, until you are left alone. Last of all, because they have to choose everybody, you are taken. "Okay, c'mon, I guess we're stuck with you."

That doesn't exactly strengthen the ego.

The apostle Paul rejoiced because God wanted him. God chose him early, "before the creation of the world" (v. 4).

To be chosen by God is exhilarating. The Jews know that. Down through history they have been honored as God's chosen people. But Paul hints here—and develops later in Ephesians—that there is a new chosen people. Not only Jews, but all who know Jesus Christ are chosen of God.

When things are tough we may be inclined to sneer, "Chosen of God? Tell me about it. Chosen for *what*? I feel more like I'm targeted."

Paul writes, "He chose us . . . *to be holy and blameless in his sight*" (v. 4). Reflect on those words. The King James Version reads, "holy and without blame before Him."

To stand before God Almighty . . . what an image! To stand guilty before *any* authority figure is one of life's harder experiences. Picture a disobedient child taken to task by his father. "Look me in the eye," the father commands, and the child shrivels.

Multiply the intensity of that experience a thousand times and you get a hint of what it would mean to stand, unholy and called to give account, before the God of the universe. Revelation 6:15-17 describes just such a situation:

> The kings of the earth, the princes, the
> generals, the rich, the mighty, and every
> slave and every free man hid in caves and
> among the rocks of the mountains. They
> called to the mountains and the rocks,
> "Fall on us and hide us from the face of
> him who sits on the throne and from the
> wrath of the Lamb! For the day of their
> wrath has come, and who can stand?"

Would you celebrate, as Paul did, the believer's "spiritual blessings in heavenly places in Christ"? Then just imagine how devastating it would be to stand—tremble might be a better word—before a holy God with your sins unforgiven; and thank him that you will never have to experience such a thing.

God For Your Father

Another imperishable asset Paul appreciated was that God has "predestined us to be adopted as his sons through Jesus Christ" (v. 5). We are not only chosen of God to stand before him holy and without blame, but we are actually members of God's family. We are his children, and we are destined to be fully revealed as such.

Again, this can best be appreciated when we look at the flip side—when we consider what we were by nature. We were children of disobedience and children of wrath (Ephesians 2:2-3). Jesus stated it even more starkly: We were children of the devil!

Paul knew what kind of person he had been, and the thought that God had adopted him greatly blessed his heart. It ought to bless us, too, for when God adopted us we were neither sweet nor lovable. But despite all our ugliness and selfishness, he adopted us into his family.

Being chosen, made holy, adopted—these were blessings Paul enjoyed by grace, blessings the world could not take away. Prison didn't make any difference. The disfavor of the ruling powers didn't matter. Paul had important things and they made his life rich.[1]

In fact, Christ's blessing made Paul's life so rich that he disdained the things he had lost and called them rubbish (Philippians 3:8). The greatest loss Paul ever experienced was probably his loss of standing among his contemporaries when he became a Christian. He described that standing like this:

> If anyone else thinks he has reasons to put confidence in the flesh, I have more: circumcised on the eighth day, of the people of Israel, of the tribe of Benjamin, a Hebrew of Hebrews; in regard to the law, a Pharisee; as for zeal, persecuting the church; as for legalistic righteousness, faultless (Philippians 3:4-6).

Paul was proud of his standing, his reputation, his heritage. We shouldn't scoff at him for feeling that way. Most of us would love to be esteemed of men as Paul was before his conversion. Furthermore, the Scripture says, "A good name is more desirable than great riches; to be esteemed is better than silver or gold" (Proverbs 22:1).

Yet Paul could write, "But whatever was to my profit I now consider loss for the sake of Christ . . . for whose sake *I have lost all things*. I consider them rubbish" (Philippians 3:7-8).

Paul knew how to celebrate when he had "lost all things." He did it by focusing on the greater assets he had gained in the process.

The Richest Man in the Valley

A rich landowner named Carl loved to ride his horse Rajah through his vast estate so that he could congratulate himself on his wealth. One day while on such a ride, he came upon Hans, an old tenant farmer who had sat down to eat his lunch in the shade of a great oak tree.

Hans didn't notice the approaching horseman at first because his head was bowed in prayer. When he did look up, he said, "Oh, excuse me, sir. I didn't see you. I was giving thanks for my food."

"Hmph!" snorted Carl, noticing the coarse dark bread and cheese constituting the old man's lunch. "If that were all I had to eat, I don't think I would feel like giving thanks."

"Oh," replied Hans, "it is quite sufficient. But it is remarkable that you should come by today, sir. I . . . I feel I should tell you, I had a strange dream just before awakening this morning."

"And what did you dream?" Carl asked with an amused smile.

"Well, it wasn't all that clear, sir. You know how dreams are. It seemed there was beauty and peace and music all around, and yet I could hear a voice saying, 'The richest man in the valley will die tonight.' In fact, that was the one part of the dream that was clear, and I woke with those words on my mind."

By now the amused smile had faded from Carl's face and he was frowning.

"I don't know what it means, sir," Hans continued. "Perhaps nothing. But I thought I ought to tell you."

"Dreams!" cried the landowner. "Nonsense!" And he turned and galloped away.

"Lord, have mercy on his soul if he really is to die so soon," Hans prayed as he watched horse and rider disappear.

Carl galloped Rajah only a short distance and then slowed the beautiful Arabian to a walk. *Die tonight?* It was ridiculous, of course. No use his going into a panic. That kind of reaction was what made such predictions come true. If he went galloping like a fool through the forest, he probably would fall and break his neck. The best thing to do about the old man's dream was to forget it.

But he couldn't forget it. Die tonight? How could he, sitting perfectly safe now in his own home? He felt fine. At least he had felt fine until Hans described his stupid dream. Now he didn't feel too well.

For awhile he debated with himself about it, but finally that evening he called his doctor, who was also a personal friend. "Could you come over?" he asked. "I need to talk with you."

When the doctor arrived, Carl told him the whole story. "Sounds like poppycock to me," the doctor said, "but for your peace of mind, let's examine you."

A little later, his examination complete, the doctor was full of assurances. "Carl, you're as strong and healthy as that horse of yours. There's no way you're going to die tonight." He chuckled. "Unless you shoot yourself or something like that."

Carl didn't think his friend's remark was terribly funny.

"Look," said the doctor, "if it will make you feel any better, I'll be glad to stay awhile."

The two friends visited for an hour or so and then played cards through the night. As dawn broke, Carl thanked his friend and told him how foolish he felt for being upset by an old man's dream.

It was about 9 A.M. when a messenger arrived at Carl's door. "It's old Hans," the messenger said. "He died last night in his sleep."

The richest man in the valley had not been the one with vast holdings, but the man of simple faith in Jesus Christ. It's a story to remember when you think you've lost everything.

Losing All the Way Around

Let's face it. I am frankly trying to be as positive as truth will allow. I'm looking on the bright side and hoping my readers will do the same.

I believe my theme, that we can celebrate when things are tough. It's time to admit, however, that not everyone will find it to be true. Sure, Hans could celebrate. Though poor in this world's goods, he was rich in faith. But what of those who have neither the benefits of this world nor the hope of heaven? What of those who are losing out all the way around?

Christina Rossetti caught the pathos of such a sorry state:

> Unthinking, idle, wild and young,
> I'd laughed and danced and talked and sung,
> And proud of health, of freedom vain
> Dreamed not of sorrow, care, or pain.
> Ah! then in those bright hours of glee,
> I thought the world was made for me.
>
> But when the hour of trial came,
> And sickness shook my feeble frame,
> When folly's gay pursuits were o'er,
> And I could sing and dance no more,
> Ah! then I thought how sad 'twould be,
> Were only this world made for me.

If you have only this world, and it turns sour, you are poor indeed. Looking on the bright side cannot help—there is no bright side. No one can—or should—celebrate when things are that dismal.

Still, one hope remains.

Paul wrote of that hope. "For you know the grace of our Lord Jesus Christ, that though he was rich, yet for your sakes he became poor, so that you through his poverty might become rich" (2 Corinthians 8:9).

Did you get that? You can "become rich."

It is actually possible for you, even if you are dead broke spiritually, to open a valid account right now in the Bank of Heaven. A rich man has made provision for his assets to be credited to your account.

It wasn't easy.

He had to go through a personal humiliation to arrange it. But the fact is that if you will apply to God now for a joint account in heaven with Jesus Christ, *your application will be approved*. And you can draw on that account from now on and never exhaust it. You will never be broke again.

How do you open the account? It's simple—just apply to God.

Here's a summary of the account waiting for you:

God so loved the world that he gave his one and only Son, that whoever believes in him shall not perish but have eternal life (John 3:16).

Go ahead. God is "in," and he's ready to take your application.

NOTES

1. Part of this chapter is adapted from the author's book: *What Makes You So Special?* (Grand Rapids: Baker Book House, 1977).

9
When Death Stalks Loved Ones

Why Die?

Today's mail brought two images of death.

First came word that my friend Janice, who had been ill with a debilitating ailment for some months, "goes in for surgery to remove at least five lumps—the biopsies showed malignancy."

Janice is a young wife, a mother of two children, a writer just coming into her prime. Less than a month ago, she called to tell me the happy news that a major publisher had accepted her first book manuscript. Now . . .

I know that cancer isn't always fatal, but the news makes me fear for Janice. *She's too young to die,* my heart protests.

Yet another letter in the mail is from Diana, a young woman I met at a conference only a few weeks ago. She pours out her grief concerning the loss of her son, who died of cancer on his birthday at the tender age of one year. She writes:

> I didn't even know babies could get cancer when our eight-month-old son was

diagnosed with hepatoblastoma—a malignant liver tumor. It was inoperable and the disease had already spread to his lungs. The doctors told us that no child with this type of cancer had been known to survive.

They assured us that the tumor was caused by nothing we had done or had neglected to do. It was neither hereditary nor contagious. Because such a large portion of his liver was involved by the time he was eight months old, they suspected he had been born with the malignancy.

Inwardly, I raged.

Why, God? I thought you took care of infants in the womb. I did my part. I ate right. I had good prenatal care. I prayed every day for the new life forming inside me. We publicly dedicated him to you soon after he was born. *Why?*[1]

The Believer's "Rights"

Diana firmly believed in divine healing. Only recently she embraced much teaching on the believer's "rights." Healing was to be claimed by faith. She concluded that the cancer was God's way of testing her faith, and she determined to meet the test. "God is going to heal my son," she told the doctors and nurses. "You'll see."

For three months Diana refused even to consider the possibility her son might die. That would be a lack of faith. Meanwhile the child continued to deteriorate. He refused all food except breast milk. Diana stayed with him in the hospital around the clock, ready to feed him anytime he would eat. He only grew sicker, and then began bleeding internally.

As I stood by his crib, I poured myself out in prayer and I felt the Lord speak to me. "Let not your heart be troubled: ye believe in God, believe also in me." The words comforted me until I looked them up in John 14 and read the next verse. "In my Father's house are many mansions: if it were not so, I would have told you. I go to prepare a place for you."

Diana resisted the obvious implication of the words. God was going to heal her son. She had declared it to everyone.

The next day the child went into a coma. He never saw the cupcake with one candle that the cafeteria prepared for his birthday. Nor the huge, stuffed green frog the volunteer brought. His body had begun to retain fluids and his tissues swelled like a lumpy balloon. A respirator breathed for him.

Two doctors ushered us into the conference room that evening. "We are doing everything we possibly can," they assured us, and they listed their recent efforts. "He has suffered brain damage by this time and will never again be normal," they said, preparing us for the worst.

"I can't bear anymore," my heart cried out to God. "Why, why, WHY don't you just heal him now? Please God!"

"You must give him to me."

"No, Lord. That would be lack of faith."

Immediately, Diana was struck with the error of her thinking. If she genuinely believed God, she would not try to tell him what to do. She must trust him. "All right. All right. I give him to you," she said.

Diana truly expected that God would now raise up

her dying son. She had surrendered to God, just as Abraham had when asked to sacrifice his beloved son, Isaac. This would now be a tremendous miracle that the medical staff could not deny.

One hour later the child died.

Anger and Confusion

Diana was angry. "Now you've really done it," she complained to God. "For anyone else, I'd ask that you bring him back to life, but you know I can't ask that for my baby after he has tasted the joys of heaven and freedom from pain."

The next days were excruciating for Diana.

> My breasts swelled hard with milk and burned with pain. Medication to stop milk production failed to help. But the physical pain was nothing compared to how badly I hurt inside. It was as though a part of my heart had been ripped out by the roots and I was left bleeding, hollow, aching. I had no idea grief could be so devastating.

Wounded, confused, Diana prayed for daily strength and comfort. At the same time she cowered in fear of another blow. How could she be sure what to expect from God anymore?

A passage in John's gospel impacted her deeply. The disciples were complaining about a "hard saying" of Jesus which they didn't want to accept. Many turned back from following him.

"You do not want to leave too, do you?" Jesus asked the Twelve.

Simon Peter answered, "Lord, to whom shall we go? You have the words of eternal life" (John 6:67-68).

Though her questions remained and her heart ached,

Diana resolved she could not turn back from following Jesus. She simply had nowhere else to go.

Jesus—Our Only Hope

It is ever thus. Because Jesus Christ is within us and there's nothing but a spiritual void without him, we hang on. We get through the hard times. Eventually, blue skies again stretch over our heads, and life is good.

No "answers" will take us through life's hard times. It is not *what* we know but *whom* we know that is critical to our survival. It is Christ who is our Rock. It is in Christ we can do all things. He is the beginning and the end.

And yet . . .

Diana might have suffered less if she had understood more. There are helpful attitudes, and there are harmful misconceptions.

Death Versus the Rights of the Believer

Jesus conquered sin and death once and forever through his own death and resurrection. He defeated Satan and purchased our redemption. Nothing remains to be added to his finished work on our behalf. We must simply claim by faith what he offers us. Satan is defeated, and it is tragic for us to continue to be bullied by him.

All of this is true. The Bible also makes it clear, however, that our redemption is not yet complete regarding our physical bodies.

Perhaps no passage of Scripture throbs with the "rights" of the believer more than Romans 8. From the "no condemnation" of verse 1 to the "nothing can separate us from the love of God" in the last verse, it is a celebration of what it means to belong to Christ.

Yet in the middle of this proclamation of the believer's blessings is a word that some fail to hear.

¹⁸I consider that our present sufferings are not worth comparing with the glory that will be revealed in us. ¹⁹The creation waits in eager expectation for the sons of God to be revealed. ²⁰For the creation was subjected to frustration, not by its own choice, but by the will of the one who subjected it, in hope ²¹that the creation itself will be liberated from its bondage to decay and brought into the glorious freedom of the children of God.

²²We know that the whole creation has been groaning as in the pains of childbirth right up to the present time. ²³Not only so, but we ourselves, who have the firstfruits of the Spirit, groan inwardly as we wait eagerly for our adoption as sons, the redemption of our bodies. ²⁴For in this hope we were saved. But hope that is seen is no hope at all. Who hopes for what he already has? ²⁵But if we hope for what we do not yet have, we wait for it patiently.

Suffering Now, Glory Later

Observe from the foregoing passage: We *do* experience "present sufferings" (v. 18). We are not exempted from pain because we are Christians. This suffering, we are told, is not only small compared to our future (note *future*) glory, but it is so small as to be not worth comparing. Note too that this all-surpassing future glory is to be revealed *in* us, not *to* us.

Something glorious is going to happen in us because we are Christ's—but it hasn't happened yet! So we wait, along with all of creation, "for the sons of God to be revealed" (v. 19).

We became sons of God when we received Christ as savior (see John 1:12). We are already—right now—God's children. But our sonship is not yet fully revealed.

What still needs to happen for us to be revealed as sons of God? For what change are we still waiting?

The passage answers that question. "We wait eagerly for our adoption as sons, *the redemption of our bodies*" (v. 23).

Our bodies are not yet redeemed. That's why they get worn out and sick, and that's why they die.

Paul wrote elsewhere about this change in our bodies that we await. "We will be changed. For the perishable must clothe itself with the imperishable, and the mortal with immortality. When the perishable has been clothed with the imperishable, and the mortal with immortality, *then* the saying that is written will come true: 'Death has been swallowed up in victory'" (1 Corinthians 15:52-54).

Note the *then,* the future aspect to all of this.

Then "the creation itself will be liberated from its bondage to decay" (Romans 8:21). At the present time, our bodies, along with all the creation, are still in bondage to decay.

That's what happened to Diana's son. That's what is happening to my friend Janice. That's what is happening to you and to me. We all occupy bodies that are in bondage to decay. We are all dying. We can slow the death process, and we should. We can turn back, for a time, the assaults on our bodies. But the outcome is not in doubt.

This might be depressing, but it is the truth.

Jesus said, "I am the truth." He will not deceive us about life in order to make us feel better for a little while. Diana's little while of feeling better, based on false hopes, cost her dearly when the truth proved unyielding.

Nevertheless, we have abundant hope. In a short while our blessed Lord will banish death forever.

But we have something else besides hope; we have

power. As we echo Peter in saying to Jesus, "To whom shall we go? You have the words of eternal life," He replies to us, "I will never leave you nor forsake you." He is always with us, for he indwells us. He will be with us through every battle, including the last one with death. He will stay with us and bring us out whole on death's other side.

How can we say anything but "Thank you, Jesus!"

NOTES

1. Diana Savage Kruger, unpublished manuscript, 1984.

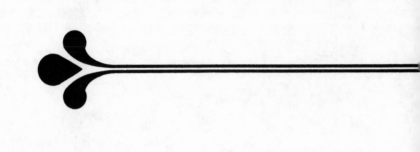

10
When You Face the Last Enemy

Death's Long Shadow

I was seven years old when I had my first personal encounter with death. At Easter, my brother Ron and I each received a real live bunny from our parents, along with a warning: "Be careful playing with them out in the yard. If a dog comes along, it may kill them. So watch out."

I didn't take the warning lightly. My imagination painted a vivid picture of my furry little rabbit being ripped to shreds by the sharp teeth of a marauding dog.

On a sunny afternoon a few days later, Ron and I took our bunnies into the side yard and put them down between us on the grass. We had enjoyed them only a few minutes when a dog trotted by on the sidewalk in front of our house.

"A dog!" Ron cried in alarm.

I jumped to my feet. No dog was going to get my rabbit. I would see to that. I'd chase him away. I took one quick step toward the sidewalk, and my foot came down with all my weight right on my rabbit.

I crushed the insides out of the little animal and I

knew it was as good as dead. That day I got my first demonstration of death's power. Try as I might to defeat it, death had triumphed. My best efforts had not only failed to preserve life, but had destroyed it.

"*There's Nothing We Can Do*"

I was barely eleven when my father died of Bright's disease. He was stricken on Christmas Day and lay in a coma until December 28, my sister's birthday. I couldn't understand it. He was in the hospital. The doctors knew what was wrong with him. Yet they were letting him die.

"There's nothing we can do," they said. "His kidneys are gone. It's just a matter of hours."

I previously had decided I would be a doctor. That call seemed certain from the day my mother took me to see a doctor for bedwetting and he charged *two dollars* for simply talking with us a few minutes. *Wow, that's for me*, I thought. *What easy money!*

Now I knew that I would never be just another helpless doctor. I would do medical research. I would find a cure for Bright's disease. Nobody should ever again have to hear those despairing words, "There's nothing we can do."

Sin Is the Real Killer

I never became a doctor or a medical researcher. In my teens, I came to know Christ. Then I realized it was sin that killed my father—perhaps directly because his lifestyle aggravated his condition, but at least indirectly because death had entered the world through sin. If I were to fight the real killer, I would have to focus on sin, not on disease. And if I wanted to fight sin effectively, I could best do it by witnessing of Christ, who had already provided the remedy for sin.

Although (or perhaps because) death cast its long shadow over my life early, I have never been able to get used to the idea. I don't understand how some people seem to take death for granted . . . as if it should be expected . . . as if it were *natural*.

My rabbit should not have died; it was all a grotesque blunder on my part.

My father should not have died; it was a failure of medical science, or it was wrong choices on his part, but it was NOT "The Plan." He was only forty-six. I was only eleven. I needed him. His death was just plain *wrong*.

I know that some will say I'm letting my heart do my thinking instead of my head. The food chain depends on one animal eating another, and so does the balance of nature. Furthermore, sheer population control requires death.

I'm also aware that some would say, "Aha! Now we know why you are so religious. You can't accept the reality of death, so you deceive yourself through Christian faith; you make death an illusion."

Death Is Real, but Not Essential

Not so. Death is very real. I have no doubt of that. But why must I see it as essential? The universe has planets like the sands of the sea for number—and I'm supposed to think that population control is an insurmountable problem? Why let my thinking be confined to the circumstances in which nature exists at the moment? God is quite resourceful enough to manage a universe without death.

True, it's my heart that first protests against death as an unnatural intruder into human existence. But my head can grant that possibility as well!

So I continue to protest, although for now death gets the last word. Not every attempt to ward off the dogs of death leads directly to disaster, but something always kills the rabbit. Medical science today has dialysis machines for kidney patients, and can even transplant healthy kidneys into someone who would otherwise die, like my father. But sooner or later, the doctor still tells everyone, "There's nothing we can do."

Realizing Our Own Mortality

We all know we are going to die. It's the ultimate human statistic. One out of every one living person dies, 100 out of every 100, and 1,000 out of every 1,000. (Enoch and Elijah are exceptions, but two out of the earth's billions are statistically insignificant.)

Sigmund Freud and others have argued that we do not grasp that we are going to die and that, in fact, our own death is unimaginable to us. When we think of death, it is of another's death. Or of the death of some part of ourselves.

Existentialists, by contrast, argue that death is the one absolute in life and that confronting the fact of our own death gives reality to life. I am convinced that the fact of our own death is the context in which each of us lives out his or her days. Death overshadows and colors all that we do—even when, as is often the case, denying death is the mode in which we operate.

Why does the teenager want to "live it up" unless he senses that he does not have forever? He not only knows that everyone dies, but he also knows that he personally is on a time track that never can be reversed. He is traveling from birth to death, and anything he misses along the way is lost.

Why must a person get his training, begin his career, raise his family, all in timely fashion? Why does a sense of urgency strike young adults to make them feel they must be executive vice-presidents (or whatever) by the time they are thirty-five?

Why does the person in midlife often face a crisis? He may panic over lack of progress . . . and then despair. Is it not because death is keeping a faster pace than he? Death mocks him and declares that he will never do or be all that he once hoped.

We are in a race and our opponent is death. Time is not the opponent, as we may be inclined to think. Time wouldn't mean anything if we weren't trying to outrun death. We could learn tomorrow, travel tomorrow, play tomorrow, love and work and serve God tomorrow. It's knowing that death will someday deny us another tomorrow that forces us to strive now. We not only may but we must "grab for the gusto." We are not free.

When Hebrews speaks of "those who all their lives were held in slavery by their fear of death," it means all of us (see Hebrews 2:15).

Overcoming the Fear

People fear death because it means an end to their earthly lives. But they also fear it because of what may come afterward. It would be nice to affirm that those who believe in God have little or no such fear . . . yet that is not necessarily so.

Secular studies of how "religion" affects one's fear of death are interesting but inconclusive. Some studies have found religious people are more afraid of death than the nonreligious. Other studies have found just the opposite. Several studies of each kind are reported in "Fear of Death and Dying," by Glenn M. Vernon.

Dr. Vernon suggests a possible explanation for this conflicting data: "Apparently what might have happened to individuals who evidence high fears of death is that, from the whole configuration of 'you are evil—you can be religiously saved' teachings to which he was exposed, the 'you are evil' aspect was given the greatest saliency."[1]

This suggestion makes sense. If what you hear and believe is that you are evil and will face the judgment of a holy God after death, it's no wonder you fear death. But if you hear and believe that you are reckoned perfectly righteous in Christ and will be welcomed into glory by a loving heavenly Father, fear has nothing on which to feed.

Those of us who minister in the name of God need to ask ourselves which message our listeners are getting. The gospel is a message of forgiveness, of reconciliation, of peace with God through our Lord Jesus Christ. Warnings to the unrepentant and unbelieving are biblical, too, but the salient message for those who respond must be, "Go in peace, you are fully accepted in Christ."

The happy news of the gospel does not at all mean, however, that true believers welcome death. Other factors besides being saved affect our outlook. We still have to concern ourselves with the experience of death itself, and about the termination of our earthly ties and opportunities.

Fulfilling Your Destiny

Sometimes my thoughts about my own death arrange themselves into a guessing game. I was aware as a young man that, while I could die any day, the chances weren't great. I was at very low risk of death by disease, and only moderately endangered by accidents.

Now middle-aged, I know that my chances of dying soon are greatly increased. I need only look at insurance premium charts to realize it. Rates are perhaps double for a forty-year old what they are for a twenty-year old. They really start climbing at fifty (three times as much) and spurt to ten times as much at age sixty.

But I am me. I am not a statistical average. I have good habits. I don't drink, smoke, or grossly overeat. I'm not excessively driven by ambition. I don't worry much. I know how to handle stress. Most of my predecessors on my mother's side died at advanced ages, as did many on my father's side (excepting the considerable number who opted for hard living).

None of my advantages are guarantees, of course. So when I get sick or sense danger or have pains now, I am likely to wonder, *Hmmmm, could this be it?*

I indulge sometimes in a bit of speculation as to just how and when I will die. Will I outlive most of my contemporaries and die by imperceptible degrees, the last of my generation to check out long after any good reason to live on has disappeared? Sometimes I think that's likely.

But I could be stricken by a fatal disease. Sickness could devastate and ultimately destroy this body that has served me so well up until now. I may have to go through the anxiety of wondering what my disease is, dreading it, hoping it's not serious, and then being disappointed, and all the time fighting to live.

Then again, maybe I will go suddenly in an accident or with a heart attack, leaving family and friends to reel with shock, wholly unprepared for my death. It could happen.

And so I feel like a detective without the clues I need to solve a mystery that will one day be so clear that it will seem the story could hardly have ended any other way.

As I intimated earlier, I didn't view my own death in this almost whimsical fashion twenty years ago. Even now, you shouldn't assume that I'm prepared to go peaceably. Not at all. I'm just somewhat less angry about the possibility of my dying than I used to be.

Circumstances Change Viewpoints

Much of my mellowing attitude can be explained by changed circumstances. Twenty years ago, my five children were aged two through fifteen, and they needed me. Even more compelling than that, I hadn't fulfilled my calling. I had a sense of mission from God—to make my life count for something in his service.

Now the children are full grown, and I believe I have to some degree fulfilled my calling, mostly through writing.

I think I see in Paul a pattern of change similar to what I've just described. He once wrote that to choose between living and dying was difficult for him. "I am torn between the two: I desire to depart and be with Christ, which is better by far; but is is more necessary for you that I remain" (Philippians 1:23-24).

My guess is that earlier, in the first years after his conversion, Paul would have felt differently. Not yet having begun to energetically fulfill his destiny, he would have viewed his death as untimely (see Galatians 1:15).

Late in life, however, he was fully prepared to go. "The time has come for my departure," he wrote. "I have fought the good fight, I have finished the race, I have kept the faith" (see 2 Timothy 4:6-7).

If you are a Christian and have a sense of the call of God on your life, you are probably in one of three states of destiny fulfillment:

You have hardly begun.

You have served the purposes of God
    for your life but still have much to offer.

You have pretty much completed your work.

You will view your own possible death differently from each of these stages, regardless of your age.

Always an Enemy

Just because Paul was more receptive to the prospect of dying after he had finished his course, it does not follow that he liked the idea. Paul called death an enemy, and he never did change his mind and cozy up to his grim adversary.

Certainly some people desire to die. They say, and really feel, that death would be a welcome release from their suffering. This is not because death has ceased to be an enemy, but because death is winning the conflict and they have lost hope.

Such a person feels that his dying cannot long be suspended, so let it at lease come to a conclusion. Let the battle end with his own negotiated surrender rather than his utter defeat.

People speak of dying with dignity, by which they mean under conditions that permit them to influence the way they die, rather than allowing death to entirely humiliate them.

This dying as a last act of defiance can be seen in the condemned criminal who commits suicide. Special precautions are often taken to keep the condemned from taking his own life and thereby "cheating the executioner."

King Saul died by his own hand when the tides of battle turned against him and his death became inevitable.

Death is always our enemy. It is linked in Scripture with two other implacable foes of man: sin and Satan. "The wages of sin is death" (Romans 6:23). "The thief (Satan) comes only to steal and kill and destroy" (John 10:10).

Jesus is our savior from sin and Satan and death. But as we observed in the previous chapter, the redemption of our bodies has not yet occurred. Jesus "must reign until he has put all his enemies under his feet. The last enemy to be destroyed is death" (1 Corinthians 15:25-26).

Experiencing Death

People who have had "near-death" experiences have been the subject of various popular books and television reports in recent years. Most such people, Christian or not, have reported positive, happy experiences.

Helmut Thielicke in *Living with Death* points out that as early as 1938 a French doctor named Barbarin argued in his book *Death As a Friend* that death is a pleasant experience. All the pain and anxiety and turmoil common to the predeath state disappear and the dying person feels euphoric.

Thielicke comments:

> What seems to me to be dubious about the subject matter of these works on the experience of death is the effort to reduce the problem of dying to the last hour of life and therewith to rob it of its character as a sign of our finitude. Awareness of the destiny of death as the constant companion of the whole of life is here suppressed. One might say that the existential character of our dying and our awareness of mortality are eliminated. Whereas death is relevant here only as an event of the last hour, the Christian understanding of death as the "last enemy" has always regarded it as the shadow cast over the whole of existence and as a power that accompanies existence over its whole temporal length.[2]

As we have already observed, death is not only a last hour phenomenon. Its shadow looms over all preceding life, and it permanently changes whatever existence follows it. Nevertheless, death itself is of interest to everyone, since we must all pass through it.

Reports of pleasant deaths may encourage us, but as Christians we have something more. I offer as illustration an experience of my own.

A Companion in the Darkness

I was not apprehensive when I made plans to take gas for a tooth extraction. I was happy about the idea. When the soft rubber mask covered my mouth and nose and the nurse-anesthetist began humming softly, I wondered curiously just how long it would take for me to go "out."

A big light shining in my face became my focus as the outer edge of my vision began to darken. The circle became smaller with every breath until there was only a dot of light in the center. And then—total darkness.

Now I'm out, I thought. But the mask remained over my face and the darkness deepened. What's the matter with her? I thought. *Doesn't she know I'm already out?* Panic hit me.

This crazed woman is going to kill me!

My mind whirled. *I've got to hold on,* I thought, struggling against the effects of the gas.

"No, I'll hold on to you."

The voice was from Someone closer than hands or feet, and I knew it was the Lord.

I relaxed, and the next thing I knew I was laughing at something I thought hilariously funny. I was coming to and I couldn't wait to ask the dentist, "Are you sure you pulled the right tooth?" My great amusement was an effect of the "laughing gas" anesthesia.

I believe Jesus will be present when we come face to face with death, just as he was with me in that dentist's chair.

Thielicke writes, "We go down into death with empty hands, with no substance of the soul that is sheltered from death, and can only beg God to hold us fast." From our viewpoint, that may be true, but I don't think we will do any begging. Jesus will be there, even unbidden, to assure us that he will never let go of us.

This special presence of the Lord is suggested by the language of the twenty-third psalm. The psalm talks first *about* the Lord. "*He* makes me lie down in green pastures, *he* leads me beside quiet waters" (v. 2 NASB). But then death approaches and the psalmist begins to talk not about the lord, but to him. "Even though I walk through the valley of the shadow of death, I fear no evil, for thou art (not 'he is') with me" (v. 4).

Killed but Not Hurt

Because the Lord was with him, the psalmist feared no evil (or *no harm*, as it might be translated). That's beautiful. We may not be able to escape death, but we can escape harm.

Jesus taught much the same thing in a rather curious discourse to his disciples. In warning them of the persecution they could expect, he said, "You will be betrayed by parents, brothers, relatives, and friends, and they will put some of you to death. All men will hate you because of me. But not a hair of your head will perish."

What's this? We may die but we won't lose any hair? We won't lie bald in our caskets? Who cares? Frankly, that's small comfort to me.

But Jesus is really saying that even if we are killed, he will see to it that we are not in the slightest harmed.

But what does that mean—not harmed?

More Than a Body

I talked with Janice again lately, the friend I mentioned in the previous chapter who only recently learned she has cancer. She didn't have the surgery to remove the malignant lumps. The doctors said the cancer has spread all through her body and is inoperable.

As the doctors explained the results of their tests and

showed Janice the blips indicating cancer in various organs, she had a certain sense of detachment. Her body was racked with cancer, but *she* was deeper. Her body was apparently dying, but *she* would live.

I read this chapter to Janice and to the others in our critique group. "There is much more about death I could say, but my aim is not so much to fully discuss death as it is to help readers get through the hard time of facing death or bereavement," I said.

"I think it's right on target," said Janice. "I've already come to most of those same conclusions. But what is hardest for me . . ." She paused and her eyes glistened with tears. "What's hardest is leaving my family . . . not because of my loss but theirs, especially the children. I don't want them to be bitter because their mother was taken away from them."

Another member of the group, Gloria, cited Isaiah 40:11 (NASB): "Like a shepherd he will tend his flock, in his arm he will gather the lambs, and carry them in his bosom."

"The Lord will take special care of your children, Janice," she said, "and they can become all the stronger for it."

I recalled how, years ago, my Bible teacher had been concerned that his frequent ministry away from home could be detrimental to his children. Once he commented to a friend, "If my children grow up to follow the Lord, it will be only by the grace of God."

The friend answered, "If your children grow up to follow the Lord, it will be only be the grace of God *whether you are there or not.*"

We're Never Left Alone

It is wonderful that Jesus goes with us through the valley of death and out to the other side. But wonder of wonders, he also remains here to tenderly guide and guard those we must leave behind.

So Jesus—blessed Jesus—is the One who will get us through every other test.

We may lose everything, but he is still there.

We may not understand his dealings with us and be hurt or angry with him, but he is still there.

We may fail the Lord so grievously that we can hardly forgive ourselves, but he is still there.

We may feel dead inside and have no sense that God is *anywhere*, much less within us, but he is still there.

We may be worried and unable to shake our anxiety because the threats we face are real, but he is still there.

We may be lonely and feel rejected, but he who said, "Never will I leave you; never will I forsake you" (Hebrews 13:5) is still there.

We may feel confused and lost because life as we have known it has disappeared and the ground we stood on vanishes, but he is still there.

As long as there is a *you*, he will still be there. And as long as he is there, you will be all right.

"For in him dwelleth all the fullness of the Godhead bodily. And ye are complete in him" (Colossians 2:9-10 KJV).

Complete. Entire. Whole.

He has promised, and so shall we be.

Forever!

NOTES

1. Glenn M. Vernon, "Fear of Death and Dying," in *Sociology of Death* (New York: The Ronald Press, 1970), p. 197.

2. Helmut Thielicke, *Living with Death* (Grand Rapids: Wm. B. Eerdmans, 1983), p. 19.

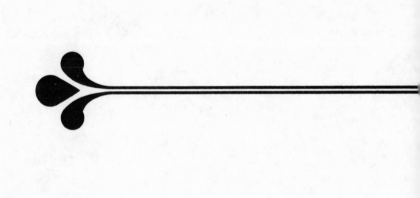

Part 3

Getting Over the
Hurt of Being Human

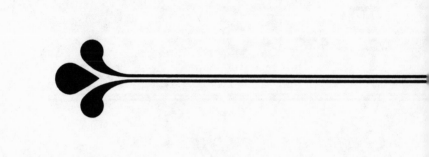

11
When You Have Been Wronged

Gut-Level Hate and Love

One after another they came, people who had been done dirt and who were more than willing to tell about it. I had announced at the close of a singles meeting that I was writing this book and that I wanted to speak with those who had been seriously wronged. As I expected, many of their complaints were against former spouses.

There were the usual: "My husband left me for another woman, and after I gave him the best years of my life."

And there were variations. Joy's husband had left her and their three children after twenty-four years of marriage—not for another woman, but for a man. He announced that he was gay, and though he "loved" his family, he had to go on with his own life. When it all sank in, Joy was bitter. She had been tormented all these years thinking their dismal sex life was her fault. Why hadn't he told her? He had wasted years of her life. She might have found a good marriage with someone else if he had left her at age twenty-two or thirty or even thirty-five. Now she was forty-three years old. Her chances of marrying well were diminished, and even if she did, nothing could restore the lost years.

Cindy had been robbed of her children. She had been a good mother and it never once entered her mind that her husband might win custody of the children when they divorced. Only after it was over did it dawn on her what had happened. Her lawyer was an alcoholic and incompetent. He hadn't presented her case well, while her husband's lawyer had made him look wonderful. The judge, she learned, had himself been divorced and lost his children to his wife. Shouldn't he have disqualified himself? She could appeal, could fight for custody, but that might be very destructive to the children. Cindy simply had no good way out, and she was burned up about it.

Don wanted to make it clear that women weren't the only ones victimized by ex-spouses. His ex-wife had taken him for everything he had. It wasn't as if he earned a good income while she was at minimum wage. She was an executive secretary and made more than he did. What was worse, the home they had owned free and clear—which the judge awarded to her—was his family home inherited from his parents. He had entered the marriage with money and assets; she had not. They had come out just the opposite. "I tell you, there's no justice!" said Don.

Mary asked if I'd heard how some women had worked to put their husbands through college only then to be dumped. When I nodded, she said, "Well, now you've met one."

Not all of the tales of woe related to divorce. Jane was a young widow who felt she'd been wronged by her former church. The other women treated her like a threat to their marriages. The pastor had no compassion. "Your Maker is your husband" he quoted to her from Isaiah 54. The verse was fine but the way he applied it made her feel like she was some kind of sinner for hoping ever to marry again.

Pat, a diabetic, had been mistreated by her doctor. He had failed first to treat the osteoporosis that diabetics tend to suffer. When her toes became so brittle that they broke, he denied they were broken and refused to x-ray them, cursing at her and calling her "a hysterical woman." As a result, Pat has permanently deformed toes and constant pain.

Fred was an abused child. His parents had often locked him in a dark closet for being bad. They yelled at him continually, ridiculed him, and beat him. He grew up like Rob (chapter 2) believing he was worthless but also knowing his parents were cruel. He hated both himself and them.

These were the seriously trampled-upon who were willing to tell their stories. Probably all of us have been grievously wronged at some time, or we will be. When it happens, how do we handle it? What do Christians do when somebody does them dirt?

Getting Even

Darlene Bogle was having problems with her neighbors, the Coopers. They didn't like her cat with its habit of using their yard for a litter box. One day they took matters into their own hands and killed the cat with a BB gun.

An imaginative woman, Darlene disdained ordinary tactics of revenge. She would devise something exotic.

A few days later, the neighbors had no electricity, no water, and no gas. The utility companies had simple explanations. A woman had called, identified herself as Mrs. Cooper, and ordered the services discontinued.

Only the telephone still worked; it had apparently been overlooked. Late that night the Coopers learned why. Someone had placed an ad in the local paper offering their house for sale at an unbelievable bargain price. "Call after 10 P.M.," the ad stipulated.

Darlene remembers all of this with mixed feelings. Now a Christian, she disapproves of her vengeful actions. She knows that Scripture says, "Do not take revenge, my friends, but leave room for God's wrath, for it is written: 'It is mine to avenge; I will repay,' says the Lord" (Romans 12:19).

On the other hand, she still thinks her revenge had a certain imaginative flair. But she now tries to channel her creativity into writing and speaking for the Lord.

Why Not Get Even?

Just knowing that the Lord forbids our taking revenge should be sufficient to keep us from doing it. We want to obey our Lord, whether or not we understand all the reasons for his commands. In this matter, however, the Lord wants us both to obey and to know why.

"Do not repay anyone evil for evil," we read. "Be careful to do what is right in the eyes of everybody. If it is possible, as far as it depends on you, live at peace with everyone" (Romans 12:17-18).

God doesn't want us to do evil. The fact that someone else does evil to us doesn't change that. He wants us to "do what is right," even if others do what is wrong.

As God sees it, and as we need to see it, the problem when we "get even" is that we are doing exactly that. The other person has sunk to a low level, and we are getting down there with him. If our enemy were destitute, would we want to lose our assets too and get even? If he were sick, would we want to lose our health and get even? Of course not. Then if he has done evil, why should we lose our integrity by getting even?

God says in effect, "Don't get even; come up higher." He wants us to be better people.

When we respond to God's command and forsake revenge, we save both ourselves and others a lot of grief. Darlene's actions hurt her neighbors without really helping her, and she increased the likelihood of an even more destructive retaliation from them. As Scripture says, "If you keep on biting and devouring each other, watch out or you will be destroyed by each other" (Galatians 5:15).

If Thoughts Could Kill

You have been wronged. Inside you recognize a desire to strike back, but you won't. God's Word is clear that you must not do so, and you can see some reasons why. You are over the first hurdle—but only the first, for God says you must neither take vengence *nor hold resentment*.

Here's the Scripture: "Get rid of all bitterness, rage and anger, brawling and slander, along with every form of malice" (Ephesians 4:31). Resentment can take various forms and this verse specifically mentions several. Then it sums up all of them with the expression *every form of malice*. That's comprehensive!

This is a good place to observe that "every form of malice" includes resentment toward those who have wronged us in small ways, too. While focusing on serious wrongs, we must not overlook the very real problem we can have over minor slights. The thoughts in this chapter apply to both situations.

But it may be especially different to get rid of our malice when we have been done a *lot* of dirt. Resentment can feel so legitimate. The fact that we can't take vengeance may make resentment seem all the more justified. Are we to let wrong-doers off the hook completely?

Even if we wanted to, we are not sure we could "get rid" of all malice. The feelings are deep. Can a person just tell himself not to feel resentful any more?

Getting Rid of Malice

A number of years ago God and I had to come to terms on Ephesians 4:31. I had some malice I didn't know how to get rid of, and though my complaint may seem minor compared to others, it was a real problem for me.

The church I pastored at the time seemed indifferent to my material needs. If it had been just me, I could have handled it. But I had a wife and family. It was my Christian duty to provide for them. More and more I came under the pressure of a no-win situation. If I stayed at the church, I was depriving my family for whom God told me to provide. If I left the church, I'd be abandoning a ministry to which I felt called by God.

As the situation continued, I felt more and more resentful toward the church. There was no question that they wanted me to stay. Why couldn't they see I needed more money? They knew I had a family. They knew what it cost to live. *I'd like to see them try to get by on my salary* I thought bitterly.

Then Ephesians 4:31 entered the picture. God wanted me to get rid of all bitterness. However legitimate my complaint, God said the bitterness had to go. I noticed that the original Greek expression translated "get rid" was a single word that literally means "let it be removed."

Here was hope—I didn't have to haul my resentment off somewhere. God would remove it. I only needed to let him do so. As I agreed with God on the issue, it was as if a petcock had been opened in my soul and the corrosive acid of bitterness drained out.

Thank God I obeyed the Lord, for otherwise that acid would have continued to eat away at my soul. That's the way with bitterness and malice. It destroys those who hold on to it. Corrie ten Boom saw this in those who suffered the terrible mistreatment of a Nazi concentration camp. She wrote:

Those who were able to forgive their former enemies were able to return to the outside world and rebuild their lives, no matter what the physical scars. Those who nursed their bitterness remained invalids. It was as simple and as horrible as that.[1]

In my own case, I still had my underpayment problem, of course, but I no longer resented the people. I was able to minister to them in the right spirit. Meanwhile, I considered more seriously whether the Lord might be leading me to make a change. Ultimately, I concluded that he was.

The Removal Process

Sometimes it helps to symbolize outwardly our inner spiritual transactions. To "get rid" of bitterness, to "let it be removed," you could cup it and dump it, as my friend Dale Galloway suggests.

Form your two hands into a cup. Now mentally deposit all your bitterness, anger, resentment, and ill will into the cup, along with all the slights and wrongs you have suffered. Lift your cupped hands to the Lord, then turn them over, palms down, and dump all the contents out. Wiggle your fingers so nothing will stick to them. Finally, thank God for removing all that you have dumped before him.

Feeling Compassion

You have ruled out revenge. You have agreed with the Lord to give up your bitterness and resentment. By these two choices, you have won a great victory and severely hampered Satan. He cannot use you to perform destructive acts of vengeance, and he cannot corrode your soul from within by stirring the acid of bitterness.

You have cleared two tough hurdles. Now comes a third.

Scripture follows up the admonition to "get rid of . . . every form of malice" with the command, "Be kind and compassionate to one another, forgiving each other, just as in Christ God forgave you" (Ephesians 4:32). This means you must now exhibit good will rather than ill will toward anyone who has wronged you.

Gut-Level Love

I'm particularly interested in the word translated *compassionate*. An anglicized form of the Greek here is *eusplanchnos*. The *eu* prefix means *good* or *well* and *splanchna* means bowels or innards. Literally, *compassionate* here means *good insides* or gut-level love.

Deep inside you once had bitterness and resentment. Then you let God remove it. Now he wants you to have—equally deep inside—benevolence instead of malice, good will instead of ill will, love instead of hate.

How do you get this gut-level love?

Just as we needn't strive to rid ourselves of malice, so we don't have to supply love. What we have to do in both instances is to say "yes" to the Lord. In this case we must say, "Yes, Lord, I am willing to have gut-level love toward the person who has wronged me."

As we thus inwardly submit to God's lordship, he sheds abroad his love in our hearts by the Holy Spirit. That's the dynamic behind the well-known gospel song "The Old-Time Religion." One stanza says, "Makes me love everybody," and that is exactly what it does.

Neither the removal of malice nor the bestowal of love is a once-for-all thing. As often as bitterness and hate return, we must come afresh to the Lord for healing.

Learning Gut-Level Love

While God can and will give us his supernatural love for our enemies, the Scripture also teaches that we ourselves should develop brotherly love. "Make every effort to add to your faith goodness . . . knowledge . . . self-control . . . perseverance . . . godliness . . . brotherly kindness . . . love" (2 Peter 1:5-7).

That brotherly love is never more tested than when some brother wrongs us. Two principles will help to keep our perspective straight and our brotherly love operational under such stress. We must learn these principles and learn them well.

1. We Aren't So Pure Ourselves

One reason we have trouble feeling gut-level love toward those who wrong us is that there is something of the self-righteous judge in us. We don't like to see wrongdoing go unpunished. When people sin seriously, we think they ought to pay for it. It's not ourselves we are looking out for at this juncture. We aren't asking to be avenged. We just want wrongdoers to receive their proper punishment. Our sense of fair play and justice demands it.

We think like King David did when Nathan the prophet told him how one of his subjects had committed blatant sin. Nathan reported that a certain prosperous man had stolen his neighbor's only lamb, a pet that was like a daughter to him. Though the rich man owned plenty of lambs, he slaughtered and served his neighbor's animal in order to feed a guest.

"David burned with anger against the man and said to Nathan, 'As surely as the LORD lives, the man who did this deserves to die! He must pay for that lamb four times over, because he did such a thing and had no pity'" (2 Samuel 12:5-6).

Nathan replied chillingly, "You are the man!"

David had many wives and could have had more, but

he stole the only wife of his neighbor Uriah and then arranged for Uriah to be killed in battle. David was indignant about the wrongdoing of another, but was guilty of worse things himself.

There's an old saying that the pot shouldn't call the kettle black. Sinners shouldn't label other people sinners. Most of us immediately want to reject this argument. "Of course everyone is a sinner," we say, "but we have never wronged anyone as so-and-so has wronged us." We may be convinced it is true and be vehement in declaring it.

Jesus says we are wrong.

It's God Who's Been Wronged

Christ taught that each of us has sinned far more against God than anyone has sinned against us. To illustrate, Jesus told about a man who owed his master a huge debt, more than he could ever hope to pay. The master forgave the man everything. Yet the same man refused to forgive a fellow servant a debt almost insignificant by comparison (see Matthew 18:23-30).

When we maintain that we have never much injured anyone, we forget how much we have sinned against God. We say, "Yes, but they have sinned against God, too, plus hurting us." But that is beside the point. The issue here is our attitude toward those who mistreat us. God's attitude toward us is forgiving even when we wrong him. If our attitude toward those who wrong us is judgmental, we are unlike God and invite his judgment.

This is God's perspective. We can argue if we choose. We can claim a place beside the Holy One and from our judgment seat condemn the miserable sinner who misuses us. We can imagine it is God and us versus the bad guys. But Jesus will have none of that. He says it is wicked to be unmerciful to others when we've been forgiven so much.

Read it for yourself:

Then the master called the servant in. "You wicked servant," he said, "I cancelled all that debt of yours because you begged me to. Shouldn't you have had mercy on your fellow servant just as I had on you?" In anger his master turned him over to the jailers until he should pay back all he owed. This is how my heavenly Father will treat each of you unless you forgive your brother from your heart (Matthew 18:32-35).

Forgive As You've Been Forgiven

Jesus requires that we forgive from the heart, that we exhibit gut-level love. We have been forgiven too much ever to hold anything against anyone else.

It is possible that some readers may honestly not see that they have sinned so grievously against God. But all of us have at times chosen our will over his. We have failed to obey the first commandment: To love the Lord with all our heart, soul, strength, and mind.

Although he made us and sustains us, we sometimes still use what he provides merely to please ourselves—we disregard his desire. We sin against the One to whom we owe everything. By contrast, the sins committed against us are small indeed.

We don't dare be unforgiving. Especially when we pray as Jesus taught us: "Forgive us our debts, as we also have forgiven our debtors" (Matthew 6:12).

2. Evildoers Don't Get Away with It

A second reason we don't express gut-level love toward those who wrong us is that we are too busy envying them. The Bible says, "Do not fret because of evil men or be envious of those who do wrong; for like the grass they will soon wither, like green plants they will soon die away" (Psalm 37:1-2).

We often secretly envy wrongdoers, and sometimes the secret is hidden even from us. We don't realize that the reason we are so upset is we're jealous. We'd like to do certain nasty things ourselves, but we fear the consequences. Others go out and do what we'd like to—or something far worse—and get away with it. And we're supposed to show "gut-level love" toward them?

They get their sin and forgiveness too.

A Wrong Perception of Sin

This envy comes from a distorted view of sin's true nature. We fail to see that these people get away with nothing. Sin is both corrupting and destructive. The more a person sins and the worse he sins, the more damaging the results will be in his own life . . . and beyond.

Suppose a person defies the laws of God and man to steal a deadly viper which you had on display. He has wronged you. He escapes apprehension by the law and seems to have gotten away with his crime. Two days later his swollen body is found beside the snake's cage. Is he to be envied?

Sin doesn't always kill people in two days. But if we are anywhere near as godly as we would like to think we are, we should realize that evildoers are to be pitied, not envied. They are stealing poison.

Having gut-level love toward wrongdoers doesn't mean that we wish them well in their sin. It means that we wish them well despite their sin, and we desire that they might be delivered both from their sin and its consequences. The two go together.

A Glaring Contrast

In Agra, India, in 1973, I visited the world-famous Taj Mahal. Though it was magnificent, one of the seven wonders of the world, I met a greater wonder on the same trip in the person of K. M. Usman.

Born in Agra, Usman became the first university graduate of his community and a *maulvi,* or priest of Islam. Eventually he came across a used Bible in which he read some fascinating things about Jesus, who according to Islam was one of the four major prophets of God.

One glaring contrast between Jesus and Muhammad, the founder of Islam, struck Usman. When Muhammad was persecuted, he prayed curses upon his enemies. "Perished be the two hands of Abu Lahab. . . . Soon shall he enter into the blazing fire, and his wife too, who goes about slandering. Around her neck shall be a halter of twisted palm fiber."

Jesus was treated much worse—mocked, beaten, and crucified. Yet he prayed, "Father, forgive them, for they know not what they do" (Luke 23:34 KJV).

Usman marveled. Muhammad's reaction to mistreatment was that of a natural man. Jesus' reaction could be understood only as that of the divine Son of God. Usman was converted to Christ and became an evangelist.

We know that Jesus taught during his life what he exemplified at his death. He said, "You have heard that it was said, 'Love your neighbor and hate your enemy.' But I tell you: Love your enemies and pray for those who persecute you, that you may be sons of your Father in heaven" (Matthew 5:43-44).

Jesus still calls us to be like him in this respect, to forgive our enemies, to be living examples of the divine power of the gospel of Christ.

When we do so, there is no telling who might see it and believe.

NOTES

1. Corrie ten Boom with Jamie Buckingham, *Tramp for the Lord* (Old Tappan, N.J.: Fleming H. Revell, 1974), p. 56, 57.

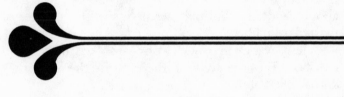

12
When God's Justice Seems Silent

Letting God Be God

Diane Bristol, aged twenty-one, was raped and murdered in 1970 in San Diego, California. Her murderer was eventually caught and sentenced to prison. In 1975 the convicted man, "Tom," received a letter from the parents of the girl. Incredibly, they were writing to express their forgiveness.

More letters and a personal visit followed. The Bristols told Tom about their faith in Christ. They said he could have forgiveness and eternal life through Christ. For a time Tom seemed responsive, but then he ended the contacts.

This was a bitter blow to the Bristols. They had hoped God could use their tragedy, and their witness, in converting the criminal. Though that has not happened, the Bristols still take comfort that God's sovereignty will cause much good to come out of the terrible evil that invaded their lives.

In her book *When It's Hard to Forgive,* Goldie Bristol writes of benefits she has already seen:

> I have learned to see God's hand at work
> through Diane's death. He has used Tom
> as an instrument to help shave off some
> rough edges in my life. . . . I know all the
> deep suffering and anguish my family and
> I have endured has helped us to grow
> spiritually.[1]

Some of those seriously-wronged singles described in the previous chapter also said God had used the mistreatment they suffered to benefit them spiritually. Losing material wealth had helped one to get eternal values straight. Losing a companion had helped another to new self-reliance and faith in God.

One of the Bible's most mistreated characters is also one of the strongest examples of how God brings good out of evil. Joseph was still in his teens when sold into slavery by his brothers. Frightened and naive, Joseph wept as he begged those heartless men not to do such a thing. They ignored him.

Years later, Joseph became governor of Egypt. He had power to execute his brothers or to save them and their whole clan from starvation. They feared he would take revenge, but Joseph saw that God had used his brothers' inexcusably wicked behavior for good. He said, "Don't be afraid. Am I in the place of God? You intended to harm me, but God intended it for good to accomplish what is now being done, the saving of many lives" (Genesis 50:19-20).

God Intends and Superintends

To say, as Joseph did, "God intended it for good" is not the same as saying you or I intend something. We intend many things that never turn out the way we'd like. "The road to hell is paved with good intentions," the old maxim says.

But God is sovereign. When he intends something to happen, it happens. God not only intends but superintends. He guides the affairs of man, including man's sins, to eventuate in a happy outcome.

The greatest example of God's superintending sovereignty is the cross of Christ. Peter told those who were party to the crucifixion, "Jesus . . . was handed over to you by God's set purpose and foreknowledge; and you, with the help of wicked men, put him to death by nailing him to the cross" (Acts 2:22-23).

The men who subjected the holy Son of God to the shameful and agonizing death of a common criminal were wicked. Yet God brought eternal life to millions by means of the worst atrocity in the history of the world.

When we've been done dirt, it helps to realize that God not only intends good to come from it, but will superintend the universe to assure such results.

God's Interpreter

Having declared God's sovereignty, we need to acknowledge that trusting in his sovereignty is not so easy when there's no possible plan to be seen and no hint of any benefit to be gained. There are cases like that, both now and from Bible times. Not every "innocent party" story reads like Joseph's.

Think of Uriah the Hittite, the victim of David's plot in the stolen lamb/stolen wife episode mentioned earlier. It's hard to see how God brought any good out of that for Uriah, even though Uriah seems to have been a decent and probably an exceptional man. Indeed, his virtue and strength of character contributed to his death when a less honorable man might have survived.

Uriah's good principles hurt him in two ways. First, they thwarted David's efforts to cover up his adultery with Bathsheba. David ordered Uriah sent home from battle for a brief furlough. He thought Uriah would surely have intercourse with his wife and would then assume that her child by David was his own. But Uriah was so honorable that he wouldn't engage in sex with his wife while his companions were embattled. David even tried getting him drunk to break down his principles. It didn't work.

Second, Uriah's trustworthy character made it possible for David to arrange something really despicable against him. David wrote a letter instructing the commanding officer, "Put Uriah in the front line where the fighting is fiercest. Then withdraw from him so he will be struck down and die" (2 Samuel 11:15).

David sent this letter back to the battlefront by the hand of Uriah himself. He knew Uriah would not steal a look at the letter. I wonder whether David may not have said under his breath, "OK, you righteous dog, you won't even sleep with your own wife, you can just carry your own death warrant to the front."

There was no justice for Uriah anywhere in this account. There was grace for David. He married Bathsheba, and she eventually became the mother of Solomon, David's successor. But Uriah seems forgotten.

Trusting in God's Grace

It is possible that you identify more with Uriah right now than with Joseph. Wrongdoers may be getting all the benefits while you in your integrity get only the shaft. You can't see one thread of good in the fabric of evil around you. If God is superintending everything to bring good out of the evil, you haven't a clue as to how.

William Cowper wrote a well-known poem that applies to such a situation. It begins:

> God moves in a mysterious way,
> His wonders to perform . . .

The fourth and sixth stanzas of the poem read:

Judge not the Lord by feeble sense,
But trust Him for His grace.
Behind a frowning providence,
He hides a smiling face.

Blind unbelief is sure to err,
And scan His work in vain,
God is His own interpreter
And He will make it plain.

I am not God's interpreter. I can't tell you why his sovereignty permits your mistreatment or how he will work it for good. But I believe that some day, even if it's in the next life, he will make it all plain.

For now, you need to trust God's sovereignty.

You need to let God be God.

Letting Dead Dogs Live

Trusting God's sovereignty is not passive resignation. It is a positive attitude that leads to positive actions. Again we see in David's life a vivid example of this principle. Only this time David was victim, not perpetrator.

Absalom, David's son, had seized the throne and forced David to flee. A man named Shimei stood beside the road down which David and his loyalists were retreating, pelted them with stones, and cursed David for "all the blood you shed in the household of Saul, in whose place you have reigned." He also said that God was judging David for that offense (see 2 Samuel 16:5-8).

This was sheer slander, for David literally bent over backward to be fair to Saul. More than once Saul tried to kill David. Nevertheless, David refused to raise a hand against Saul, even when he had easy opportunity to do so. After Saul's death, there was war between his followers and David's, but David never behaved other than honorably.

Shimei's slander angered David's long-time friend and military commander Abishai, who said, "Why should this dead dog curse my lord the king? Let me go over and cut off his head."

David replied, "My son, who is of my own flesh, is trying to take my life. How much more, then, this Benjamite! Leave him alone; let him curse, for the Lord has told him to. It may be that the Lord will see my distress and repay me with good for the cursing I am receiving today" (vv. 11-12).

We read that "David and his men continued along the road while Shimei was going along the hillside opposite him, cursing as he went and throwing stones at him and showering him with dirt" (v. 13).

Talk about being done dirt!

David believed, however, that God was in control. He even characterized the cursing as ordered by the Lord. He placed his own welfare in the Lord's hands, suggesting that God might be moved to work on his behalf to compensate for the injustice he was suffering.

David's trust in the sovereignty of God gave a constancy to his character. Circumstances change but God doesn't. When David returned to Jerusalem after the defeat of Absalom, he found a much different attitude in Shimei. "He fell prostrate before the king and said to him, 'May my lord not hold me guilty. Do not remember how your servant did wrong on the day my lord the king left Jerusalem. May the king put it out of his mind. For I your servant know that I have sinned'" (19:19-20).

Again Abishai wanted to put Shimei to death for having cursed the Lord's anointed. David said, "Should anyone be put to death in Israel today? Do I not know that today I am king over Israel?" (v. 22).

God had vindicated David. This was a time for celebration and amnesty, not bloodshed and revenge.

No Room for Revenge

So we see that David's trust in God's sovereignty left no room for revenge. There wasn't room when he was down, for God had ordained and would use those circumstances. There wasn't room when he was up, either, for God had enlarged and blessed him. Isn't that good?

Shimei's story also illustrates how persistent evildoers get their just due sooner or later. Though David never retaliated against Shimei, he did tell Solomon about the man's treachery. After David's death, King Solomon promised to spare Shimei so long as the latter remained in Jerusalem. "The day you leave . . . you can be sure you will die; your blood will be on your own head" (1 Kings 2:37).

To this Shimei agreed, but three years later he left the city to track down two runaway slaves. Solomon learned of it, summoned Shimei, and said, "Why then did you not keep your oath to the Lord and obey the command I gave you? You know in your heart all the wrong you did to my father David. Now the Lord will repay you for your wrongdoing" (vv. 43-44). Shimei was then executed.

The Sin You Can Never Forgive

We've said that letting God be God means trusting him to bring good out of evil, whether we can see any sign of that happening or not. It means adopting a positive attitude that sees him at work both when our opponents have us down and when they are at our mercy. But letting God be God means something else that we sometimes overlook: we must not borrow other people's grievances.

There is a sin you can never forgive, and that is the sin committed against someone else. You can't forgive it because you aren't the one wronged. Since you can't forgive it, you also must not "buy into" it. In other words, it is not your place to resent or revenge a wrong done to someone else (unless you have been given authority in the area). That is God's place, and you must let God be God.

Imagine with me the following scene as it might have occurred in the strategy room of Satan, the prince of darkness.

A Counsel of Darkness

"I hate meetings like this," whispered Stenchsmell as he leaned toward the fastidious figure in the next chair, jabbing his finger at the line on the agenda that announced the purpose of their meeting.

Meanmind leaned away and tried not to breathe. "Yes," he hissed, "It really stinks!" *What an incredibly clever reply,* he thought, but it was one only he would appreciate. Old Stench was as stupid as he was obnoxious.

"The meeting will come to order," said Satan, and the room became silent. "We have a task of the utmost difficulty," Satan continued. "The question before us is: How to destroy the virtuous types who seem immune to our usual vulgar tricks."

Slubgub, who sat across the table from Stenchsmell and Meanmind, stirred slightly in his chair. Pausing uncertainly after every other word, as he always did, he said, "I think—I think—I may—have stumbled—onto something—your infernal majesty."

"Stumbling would be the only way he'd get on to anything," murmured Meanmind.

Satan rapped his gavel and shot a warning look at Meanmind. "Yes. Continue, Slubgub."

"I don't know—if you'll—if you'll—if you'll—like the idea."

"Well, you never will know unless you tell us about it, now will you?" sneered Satan.

"Hmm—ah, okay—but you—but you understand —it's just—it's just—it's just—a suggestion."

Meanmind drummed the table with his fingers while Stenchsmell, in a forbidden moment of forgetfulness, rolled his eyes toward *heaven*.

"Tell us your accursed idea!" roared Satan.

"It's spelled—it's spelled—out here," whimpered Slubgub, offering copies of a memo to each member. At the top was a heading: "The Slubgub Principle," and underneath was a case history.

> Date: The year of our Enemy 1984
> Place: Scudderville, Tennessee, U.S.A.
> Category: Pastoral fight: Fourth Baptist
> Church

> Following standard procedures for sowing discord among brothers, I prompted the dismissal of two successive pastors, each of whom had considerable potential for aiding the Enemy's cause. I accomplished this despite strong opposition from a disgustingly spiritual and high-principled group of the Enemy's followers. In the midst of my campaign against yet a third pastor, I reaped a bonanza. I noticed that the righteous people, the ones opposing my work, were developing a strong sense of indignation against those I was using to oust the pastor.

> At first I didn't recognize what a marvelous opportunity that afforded me. You see, these people were the Enemy's delight and were extremely hard to subvert. Our agents had tried, believe me, but they had resisted our best ploys. Even when we incited somebody to hurt them, they followed their Master's sickening example and actually forgave those who wronged them.

At this point the reading was interrupted by a chorus of boos and groans from around the table. All were united in their revulsion. Then Slubgub continued:

> When the third pastor was ousted, these good people said they'd had enough. They denounced those I had used. They split the church. I must confess that my joy at the split was marred at first by the fear of what the new church might do to our cause.
>
> I needn't have worried. They were too filled with self-righteous animosity toward their old adversaries to do much for the Enemy.
>
> That's when I saw it. If we can get people to resent the way someone else is treated, we've got them. From a sense of fairness and love and loyalty to the wronged one, they nurture hard feelings toward the ones who have done the wrong. How's that for using good to do evil?

An Old Tactic

Satan put down the memo and a smile flickered across his lips. But only for a moment. "You fools!" he raged. "I invented this tactic long ago. Why haven't you been using it more?

"The Slubgub principle, indeed! This is straight from my old Absalom file. You devils need to study your manuals.

"Since you are so ignorant, I'll refresh your memories." Satan began his story, telling it with obvious relish. "Absalom was a disgustingly beautiful person, once. He was a son of that man I hated so, David. Absalom posed a serious threat to me, for he was a real charmer and could have led the people after the Enemy to a degree I don't even like to think about.

"I made him mine, though, by the same tactic Slub-gub here vainly imagines he has discovered. I destroyed the good man by making him hate a bad one—for a wrong done to someone else.

"Amnon was our man," Satan continued. "What a delight he was! Truly a vile, treacherous, low little weasel. He lusted after his half-sister to the point of feigning illness. He lured her into his room under the pretense of needing her care, and then forced her into sexual intercourse. After that, he ignored her pleas that he marry her to save her from disgrace.

"It was a real victory for us," said Satan, "and the best was yet to come. Absalom was outraged by what Amnon had done to his sister. I stoked his fires of "righteous anger" for two years until Absalom could kill Amnon without a twinge of conscience. In fact, he felt proud of it. Absalom became ours, and all his potential for leadership came with it. I even came close to destroying David!"

Damage Control

Although the scene I have described is imaginary, the church split and the murder were actual. (The church name and location are fictitious.) If we are to avoid adding evil to evil and falling prey to the wiles of Satan, we must resist the inclination to hate those who wrong others. We must leave the judging to the Lord. We must let God be God.

Being done wrong is a little like coming down with the measles. At best the measles are a miserable thing to have to endure. The more serious danger, however, is in the complications that may follow—inflammation of the brain, impaired vision, pneumonia. German measles can even damage one's unborn child.

If you've been seriously wronged, beware of a mind inflamed with anger, of vision so blurred that you can see neither your loving Father nor the other person clearly, of an inability to breathe free. Most insidious of all, beware of causing unseen damage to your children, including those yet unborn.

The wrong you have suffered is bound to be distressing; but it doesn't have to be disastrous. It can be turned into victory through the power of the indwelling Christ.

This Christ is the One of whom it was long ago prophesied that he would crush the serpent's head even as the serpent was striking his heel (see Genesis 3:15). The crucifixion of Jesus was the serpent's strike. But Christ delivered a final blow to Satan's head through that same cross.

The serpent, writhing in death throes, still strikes at the heels of Christ by sinking his venomous fangs into his people. His fangs may be piercing you even now.

But take courage!

"The God of peace will soon crush Satan under your feet" (Romans 16:20).

NOTES

1. Goldie Bristol with Carl McGinnis, *When It's Hard to Forgive* (Wheaton, Illinois: Victor Books, 1982), p. 161.

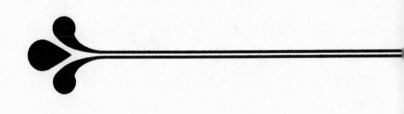

13
When You're All Alone and Blue

Sometimes Lonely Is a Good Thing

In August of my eighteenth year I set out alone to climb Mt. Hood. It is dangerous (at best) to climb Mt. Hood in August, because at that time of the year the perpetual snow fields on those steep slopes become unstable. Solitary and inexperienced climbers invite disaster.

Nevertheless, I drove to Timberline and spurning the trails beginning there, headed straight up the mountain toward its peak. "The shortest distance between two points is a straight line," I told myself.

No one knew I had gone to the mountain and I didn't bother to register at Timberline Lodge as a climber. If I had gotten into trouble, it was almost certain no one would find me in time to save my life.

Far up in the snow fields I found my ascent blocked by huge crevasses. These cracks in the ice were a hundred or more feet long, four to ten feet wide at the top, and narrowed as they plunged into blue-white depths. They also veered off at an angle as they descended. I could not tell how deep they were; it could have been 40 feet or 400.

Either way, a fall into one would mean the end.

At first I skirted a crevasse or two and kept on climbing, but I soon encountered more and more of them. So much for my straight-line-between-two-points theory. I turned to survey what seemed like the whole world at my feet. Far below, the massive lodge at Timberline looked like a child's toy. I knew no one there could even see the tiny speck on the mountainside that was me. I was absolutely alone in a world of white.

I can hardly imagine a picture that better bespeaks loneliness than an isolated figure in the middle of a vast mountain snow field. But things are not always as they appear. I was not lonely in an unpleasant sense. I felt something exhilarating, something glorious about being there.

For a few moments I drank in the splendid solitude. Then, aware that this place was not only awesome but potentially deadly, I reluctantly began my descent.

Alone Is Not the Same As Lonely

My solo visit to Mt. Hood should tell you something about me. I like being alone, going fishing alone, hiking alone, working alone. "I enjoy my own company," I say with considerable satisfaction.

On the other hand, I definitely do not enjoy being alone in a crowd. For much of my life I had felt alone in a social gathering, especially an unstructured one. I didn't mix well. The superficial chatter made me ill at ease. The talk was usually frivolous and the whole atmosphere phony. I didn't care to compete for the floor and didn't know how. So I escaped by saying, "If others want to talk so badly, let them, even if they don't have anything to say."

I learned early that being alone and being lonely are not the same thing. Since then I've learned a few more things about loneliness. There are at least three different kinds of loneliness, and they have different causes. When this is not understood, we often try to apply solutions to our loneliness that have nothing to do with its true causes. That doesn't help, of course, and it *can* hurt.

The Loneliness of Individuality

A certain loneliness is essential to one's individuality. Let me illustrate by citing three examples—one from my personal life, one from recent history, and one from Scripture.

We live in the country, and in the summertime I like to go out at night and gaze at the sky. I watch the lights of passing airliners as they seem to play among the myriad stars. I know that directly above there are perhaps 100 people bound for Portland or San Francisco, all of them oblivious of me. I see the moon, full and luminous. I hear the croaking of frogs in a nearby pond as they fill the night air with music, stopping in unison as if led by an invisible conductor.

Because nobody shares the beauty and wonder of the moment with me, I feel lonely. And then I realize that no one can share it. No one, however close to me, could participate in my awe. Talking about it would only mar the vision. But unless we communicated, we would simply be two people standing there, each one alone, neither knowing the deep wonder (or lack of it) in the other person.

I alone enter fully into the inner thoughts and feelings of my heart. The only way I can escape this loneliness is to stop thinking and feeling. To stop *being*.

The Shadow of a Machine

This "existential loneliness" involves much more than experiences of moongazing. I am alone, too, in my calling from God. No one else can answer with me concerning the purpose and meaning of my life. God is shaping me to be an individual fit for eternity, and the process is essentially One-on-one.

If I do not understand and accept this, the loneliness may become too much to bear. To escape the responsibility of this loneliness I may forfeit my very identity.

Thomas Edward Lawrence, better known as Lawrence of Arabia, rose to near-legendary fame in the early twentieth century. Born in Wales and educated at Oxford, he became a hero of World War I as leader of the Arab forces fighting on the side of the Allies. Wearing a robe like an Arab and riding a horse, he confounded the opposing Turkish forces and fired the imagination of the western world.

His identification with the Arabs became so great that he resented what he saw as their mistreatment by his own British government. He therefore refused medals of honor from both Britain and France. Yet his lonely efforts on behalf of the Arabs ultimately proved futile.

Lawrence was disillusioned. He fled his world-wide fame and abandoned his colonel's rank, changed his name to John Ross and enlisted in the Royal Air Force as a private. When exposed, he adopted yet another name, T. E. Shaw, under which he served in a lowly rank the rest of his life.

At age forty-six he was discharged from the military, an empty man who spent his time puttering around as if "there is something broken in the works . . . my will I think" (Encyclopedia Britannica). Soon afterward, he died in a motorcycle accident.

Concerning his choice to become an obscure enlisted man, Lawrence had once said, "I do it in order to serve a mechanical purpose, not as a leader, but as a shadow of a machine. . . . It is a blessing to be only a part of a machine."

To bear limited responsibility, to become an anonymous cog in an impersonal machine—it seemed wonderful to Lawrence. By biblical standards it was a tragedy. The blessing of God moves in just the opposite direction, calling us to more and more individual responsibility.

As Jesus phrased it in his parable of the talents, "Well done, good and faithful servant! You have been faithful with a few things; I will put you in charge of many things. Come and share your master's happiness!" (Matthew 25:21).

Lawrence didn't want to be "in charge of many things."

It's entirely possible that someone reading these lines may feel the same way. You may be overloaded with responsiblity. You seem to detect an absolute contradiction between the two concepts Jesus joined together. "In charge of many things" doesn't fit with "share your master's happiness." To you, "In charge of many things" equals unbearable strain.

There are many ways to relieve an overload: Get strength from the Lord . . . take better care of your body . . . find restful diversion . . . eliminate some less important stressful responsibilities. You might even withdraw from the arena temporarily.

But whatever you do, don't forfeit your calling. (This forfeiture is described under other terms in chapter 5, "When Comfort Is Worse Than Pain.") Don't give up and bury your talent. To do so is to choose a puttering, something-broken-in-the-works existence.

The Lonely Jesus

We have been describing the loneliness we must bear as individuals. Presently we will consider a third example, one from Scripture, which will bring into view another kind of loneliness. It is a loneliness we need not and should not bear, seeing that we are members one of another.

Then Jesus went with his disciples to a place called Gethsemane, and he said to them, "Sit here while I go over there and pray."

He took Peter and the two sons of Zebedee along with him, and he began to be sorrowful and troubled. Then he said to them, "My soul is overwhelmed with sorrow to the point of death. Stay here and keep watch with me."

Going a little farther, he fell with his face to the ground and prayed, "My Father, if it is possible, may this cup be taken from me. Yet not as I will but as you will" (Matthew 26:36-39).

Jesus took His disciples with him to the garden. Once there, he took three of them aside to support him in his great sorrow by both their physical presence and their prayer. This remedies one kind of loneliness. When we need human companionship, it should be there for us in the community of believers.

Notice, however, that Jesus separated himself even from these three closest friends when he fell face down alone as he poured out his soul to God. If you read on in the passage, you see that while he agonized in prayer, they fell asleep. That's how alone he was emotionally. Care as they might, and try as they would, there was simply no way the disciples could fully enter into the experience our Lord had to endure.

Those, then, are my three examples. I was alone in my awe of the starry heavens. Lawrence of Arabia, unwilling to continue alone as a leader, surrendered to an existence of mechanical puttering. Jesus agonized alone in Gethsemane even though his closest disciples were with him.

So it is with us. We are essentially alone. The famous Antarctic explorer Richard Byrd once survived for five months in a nine-by-thirteen foot hut, isolated in the frozen wastes some 123 miles away from the nearest human. He later related his experience in a book with the cryptic, one-word title *Alone*. Our individuality makes *alone* the name of everyone's book, yours and mine included.

The Potential for True Companionship

There is great loneliness in our individuality . . . but also the only potential for true companionship. Two or more people truly sharing life is the essence of togetherness. But you can't have this sharing unless you begin as separate entities. There can be no communion between shadows, no camaraderie between parts of a machine. We might say that *two requires one*.

If that's true, what are our choices?

We can accept the intrinsic loneliness of being individuals and the result (at least potentially) will be the non-loneliness that comes from true companionship with others.

Or we can flee from this loneliness—and doom ourselves to a desolation without true companionship. Two cannot come together unless each one first exists separately.

This principle—that relationship depends on individuality—applies to God as it does to man. Nobody ever came to God except as an individual. It is on that One-to-one basis that the Lord Jesus Christ calls us. He says, "Here I am! I stand at the door and knock. If anyone hears my voice and opens the door, I will come in and eat with him, and he with me" (Revelation 3:20).

That is companionship!

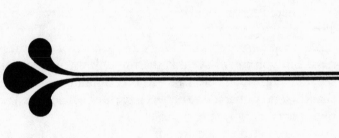

14
When You Feel Isolated and Rejected

The Loneliness No One Should Have to Bear

A few months ago we acquired a pet duck. On her first day at our place, she got out and followed a neighbor girl who was walking past on her way home from school. The duck stayed at the girl's home all night and the next morning followed her back to our place. If we had not seen the comical pair as they passed, I suppose the duck would have followed her to school.

The duck soon learned to stay close to home. She loved the frog pond, and was perfectly content there as long as someone was with her. Let us head for the house, however, and there came the duck at full waddle, trying to stay at our heels.

As she grew older "Quack Quack" (as I called her) didn't seem quite so eager for human company. She didn't always follow us. She began risking her very existence waddling around almost under the hooves of two horses in a nearby pasture. When the horses sometimes departed for greener grass, Quack Quack lived up to her name as she called desperately for her enormous friends.

That silly duck would risk her life rather than be alone.

The Loneliness of Isolation

We said at the beginning of the previous chapter that three kinds of loneliness exist. We dealt at length with one, the *loneliness of individuality*. We also touched on a second, the lack of companionship. We can call this the *loneliness of isolation*.

Abating this loneliness requires us to mix with other people, though we must remember true companionship will develop only to the degree that we (and they) avoid becoming "shadow people."

Nevertheless, there seems to be a loneliness almost biological in nature (as our duck attests). The entire animal kingdom demonstrates it; beasts do not like to be alone.

Like the animals, we may find almost any company preferable to none. Still, we often feel quite isolated and lonely if we lack quality interaction with our own kind.

A mother of small children has company enough, to be sure, but she still may long for another adult with whom to relate on an equal plane.

An older woman may have a large, extended family, but even if she lives in a rapid boil of activity, loneliness may stalk her and cause her to wish for a companion who would call her something other than "Grandma."

A single person can work with others all day, can mix socially and be involved at church, and still be desperately lonely. Flo Bryant, a Chicago-area nurse, was such a person. I first heard of Flo when, after reading a couple of my books, she wrote to ask what other books or tapes might be available. I replied, and some months later she wrote again. With her permission, I now relate the subsequent correspondence.

I'm writing to you once again to ask some questions. Maybe you can help me. If not, that's OK also 'cause I have been needing an answer for a long time.

Have you any advice for someone depressed? I have tried to talk to several people and all I hear is "it will pass." It hasn't.

I realize you are busy and it's OK if you don't have time for this. I know somewhere there is an answer. I just haven't found it yet. But I am desperate.

It's funny, but everytime I read the first pages of your book *Love, Acceptance and Forgiveness* I cry as if I had never read it before. I've never been so alone in my life as now. And, yes, I go to church every week. But it has not got what you talk about. I haven't found a church yet like you describe. If your church is like that, then the people are lucky.

Tell me, is something wrong with me to want a hug once in a while? I don't mean anything sexual. I mean a Christian hug or a touch on the arm. I can't remember when I've ever been hugged at church.

I'm depressed to the point I think death is a release. Now before you think I'm going to do anything, I'm not. But I would really welcome the release of this hell inside of me. I am at the crossroads of my life and I don't know where to go.

I believe in Jesus, I really do. But at times I need something more, if you know what I mean. This is not life. Each day is a battle to keep going. When I drive my car,

I have to be on top of myself because I find I take chances.

Pastor Baldwin, I don't know what to do. I have done all I know to do but it's not enough. Do you have any suggestions on how to fight depression? Any tapes I could buy? Anything?

The urgent tone of the letter prompted me to reply immediately. I assured Flo that nothing was wrong with her wanting a human touch or a hug. I said, "At our church and many others, the people hold hands while we pray." I suggested some books on depression for her to read and urged her to get counseling. I was also able to speak words of assurance to her from the Lord, because I sensed that she was his child and potentially complete in him (Colossians 2:10).

After many months I received a third letter, written on some positively delightful "happy" stationery. On the envelope was a heart-shaped sticker that read, "The difference in me is Jesus." Inside was a quote attributed to a J. A. Holmes: "There is no better exercise for the heart than reaching down and lifting someone up." The letter said:

I found your address and wanted to write you just because. No earth-shaking deal. Just me telling you that in the process of growing there is much pain but the end product is there.

I'm going to a Bible study on Friday where there are lots of hugs for everyone, plus some kisses for the cheeks. Where I go to church the touching is out, except for a handshake when you leave. I never knew what I was missing until I read your letter and I went searching.

I have to be honest. There is one big reason I'm still alive. For me to take my life is a sin. Every time I think about life and death, I have to measure the outcome, and as a result I'm still alive. But now I've taken some steps to help myself. I read a lot, especially the Bible. I'm going to a Christian counselor. I don't really think much has been accomplished, but I guess it all takes time.

But most of all, I'm discovering God's love. At times I just know I don't fit, and then gently I'm led to Colossians 2:10. I know that I am the only one, with Jesus, who can change myself. The sad thing is, though, I tried so long to discover God's love.

Nothing will ever change my ideas about God's love. Nothing. I still believe the end result of all the grief and heartache is healing.

I have a nurse who really has disliked me for a long time. She has even tried to get me fired. I finally had to tell her it was OK if she didn't like me, it was her problem. My problem is what I am doing about it. I don't know what I've done to her but I asked her forgiveness. She says she can't remember, just that she is mad at me. So I made it a weekend of reading and praying and asking God to help me love her. He did. Nothing has changed, but I have. I still get cut down by her and it still hurts, but it's OK.

I just need to learn more about God's love and forgiveness. Then I'll be even more better.

Well, bye, and take care. I've not met

you but I consider you my friend. Thanks.

There was one more letter. I wrote to ask if I might share her correspondence with you and she replied:

Your letter got me thinking of the ways I've been helped. For so long there really was nothing in the way of people to help. There were books, but so many said a lot of nothing.

When I wrote to you, reason told me you couldn't help, but you did by listening. I needed badly some weeks ago to talk to my pastor, and because they are in meetings, he said he was busy and it would have to wait. But, you see, I couldn't, and sometimes death doesn't wait either. So that is why I write from time to time, because even if you can't talk to me your letters tell me I'm important enough to write to.

You had suggested my going to a counselor, which I've done. I was given a test about a month ago. Do you know what it revealed? I was 90% depressed, 100% hostile, and very much submissive and ready to break. He said I was heading for a breakdown or suicide.

I have realized what I was choosing and each day it is a battle to keep going, but as you see I am still here. I'm still moving on because out of all the darkness I believe in God's love. And I learned it from books like yours. Pastor Baldwin, do you know for many like me this is the only way we get love?

In my job I've discovered I'm very able now to fully reach out and touch my pa-

tients. For the first time in months, after I
left a patient's home, I cried because she is
eighty-one and dying of cancer. I found I
really did care and the tears were real. I
finally broke through the wall a little and
it's a beginning.

There is so much in these letters, but I'll not attempt
to analyze them in order to point it all out. It is enough to
say that a once lonely, isolated, and hurting person has
been touched with the love of God. And she will soon be
touching others with that love.

The Loneliness of Rejection

There is a third major kind of loneliness. It is as-
sociated with and caused by rejection. We are likely to experience this loneliness when we are rejected by any of the
people especially close to our hearts, even if we still enjoy
acceptance by others.

Jennifer taught a women's Bible class and served as
an officer in the women's fellowship of her church. Her
husband left her for another woman, and over the next few
months she was dismissed from all ministries at the
church. The leaders said they didn't blame Jennifer for the
breakdown of her marriage. They said they would stand
behind her. But they also said she "needed time" and it
wasn't "appropriate" for her to continue in leadership.

Jennifer had heartache enough dealing with her husband's rejection—and now to feel rejected by her church
as well! "We're standing behind you," they told her. But
what did that mean? No one seemed to understand. No
one seemed to be with her. She felt desolate, alone, resentful of her rejection and guilty for that resentment.

Jim lost his job and couldn't find another. As long as
he lived, he would never forget the humiliation he felt
when he was laid off. To lose his job was bad enough, but

the insensitive way it was done . . .

One Friday at quitting time, some clerk from the office stood at the time clock handing pink slips to everyone who was being "let go." With a smirk on his face, he said, "We won't be seeing some of you fellows around here anymore."

It tore Jim up inside every time he applied for a job and didn't get hired. How desolate he felt as he walked away after each unsuccessful try, a curt "Sorry" chewing at his gut. The loneliness plagued him even as he read the want ads and saw others heading for work in the morning or returning home in the evening.

Like Jennifer and Jim, I too have experienced the loneliness of rejection. Many years ago someone I counted a friend turned against me. It came at a time when I was down already and facing severe trials. When I learned my friend was slandering me, it was almost more than I could bear.

Yet experiences like mine and Jennifer's and Jim's are mild compared to the long-term rejection and loneliness some face. Think of the lepers of biblical times, cut off from family, friends, and community. They cried, "Unclean, unclean!" to warn people away.

Think of forgotten prisoners of our own times, long since abandoned by what family and friends they ever had. Think of the deformed, who cannot be seen without a shudder of revulsion by those blessed with normal appearance.

Think of those disgraced in public office, once people of power and prestige, but now reviled.

Talk about lonely.

What to Do with It

Sometimes we over-react. When we read total rejection and personal condemnation into conditions such as being unemployed, divorced, criticized, or set aside from ministry, we may be over-reacting. Not only is loneliness eating at us, but so is self-pity.

On the other hand, I would never try to dismiss your anguish just because others have it worse. A common fault among Christians is to fall short of the love for neighbors that Jesus commanded us to practice. You very well may have suffered because of that fault.

The critical question, however, is not whether your feelings—and the treatment that provoked them—are justified, but what can you do about it?

The Strange Effect of Pets and Plants

Remember my duck? She craved my company or the horse's company—*anything* rather than being alone. Rejected and lonely people have found they, too, can get great solace from other living things when they are cut off from human companionship.

Some sense it intuitively. Whittaker Chambers went through a long and painful ordeal in the late 1940s. He was the chief witness in the government's attempts to convict state department official Alger Hiss of being a Communist spy. Chambers endured two trials, was publicly exposed as a former Communist and homosexual, and widely disbelieved in his accusations against Hiss, though the latter was finally convicted.

Chambers said afterward that the experience had made an old man of him. "It is three years," he wrote, "since I have been able to plow a field on this farm. I have sometimes thought that, if, in this coming spring, my son and I could simply work and seed a field and watch it sprout, an absolute healing would follow."[1]

Why would such a thing be so?

I think it's like this: Rejection is like water poured upon sand—it's impossible to keep from sinking in. You can fight against it, argue against it, label it unjust, but the fact remains that another human being or a society has rejected you.

You may have been at fault. You may have provoked the rejection somehow. But it doesn't help. To the contrary, it can make matters worse. Not only have you been rejected, but that judgment of you was to some degree justified.

You may find it hard to shake the feeling that you are a reject. You may wonder why you should go on living. Those who have rejected you have almost said that you shouldn't. They have written you off.

What you need is a strong word of acceptance—not from just anyone (though that would help), but from the One who counts most, from God. That's what you get when your own hands tend the soil. The seeds you plant will send up tender green shoots of new life as readily for you as for anyone else. This can be a token to you of God's love. Others have not obeyed his command to love you in spite of anything. But "He causes his sun to rise on the evil and the good, and sends rain on the righteous and the unrighteous" (see Matthew 5:43-48).

As you tend your plants day by day, you will sense that you and God are partners in this work. In Eden the first man was assigned this very activity—to dress and tend the garden. You are still God's creation, made in his image, object of his love and care.

The Animal Factor

Years ago a Christian leader known for his piety described what he recommended for people he judged were overstressed. "I tell them to go back home to the farm, wiggle their toes in the sand, and feed the chickens," he said.

That didn't sound like a very spiritual prescription to

me, but it did stick in my mind. And when I've needed it, I have found the principle very beneficial.

To those in extreme loneliness, the companionship of an animal can be virtually everything. Vera Figner spent many years alone in a prison cell. At length she befriended a little bird that flew to the barred window of her cell. The bird became tame enough to eat from her hand and to perch on her shoulder. It took up residence with her, became her cellmate. When it died, Vera wept for two weeks. She mourned that bird as we would mourn a loved one.

The Bible says, "All kinds of animals, birds, reptiles and creatures of the sea are being tamed and have been tamed by man" (James 3:7). Your potential choice of animal company is a wide one. Dogs and cats are favorites, of course, though some say cats are too aloof. One man said he preferred pigs because, "Dogs look up to you and cats look down on you, but pigs treat you as equals."

When you have been rejected, you need to be looked up to—so get a dog! The unqualified acceptance a dog offers can be affirming any time, no matter how successful or sophisticated you may be. The noted German theologian Helmut Thielicke writes concerning his pet dachshund, "I know that if something would happen to me, that your canine heart would be affected. You notice at once if something is bothering me. And if I am happy, then you make the most droll attempts to show me that you rejoice with me. . . . Our lives are more fully linked than I can say or you can bark."[2]

Getting the Strength to Reach Out

This "linking" of which Thielicke writes is exactly what a person needs who has become *unlinked* and lonely because of rejection. The linking process is precisely the means to reconnect an alienated person with others. Once we have reached out to a dog or other pet and made a friend, we are strengthened to reach out to the least threatening of our fellow humans in the same way. We realize there must be some people who are as good as dogs, people who will accept us, who will care about us, who will be enriched by our friendship.

We may want to begin with other "little" people, those society tends to neglect, such as the elderly, children, the poor. When we reach out to these people, we will be twice blessed because we help them and ourselves.

As for helping ourselves, becoming linked and staying linked to other people can actually save one's sanity. Samuel Johnson said, "Solitude is dangerous to reason, without being favorable to virtue." Vauvenargues probably expressed a better balance when he said, "Solitude is to the mind what fasting is to the body, fatal if it is too prolonged, and yet necessary." Both saw serious danger in too much solitude. Your own observation probably bears out the fact that people who are alone too much become odd.

The Christian, of course, is never really alone in the absolute sense. Our Lord not only stays with us but he indwells us. Nothing can separate us from him.

A Disappointed but Confident Apostle

One of the saddest passages of Scripture is also one of the most reassuring. It seems to me unspeakably sad that the apostle Paul should write, "At my first defense, no one came to my support, but everyone deserted me. May it not be held against them" (2 Timothy 4:16).

Here is a man who literally poured out his life and soul for others over many years. Thousands had come to know Christ through his ministry. He had blessed multitudes so that, if they could have done so, they would have plucked out their eyes and given them to him (see Galatians 4:14-15).

Now Paul is old. He is on trial for his life. The prospect of being thrown into an arena to be torn to shreds by a lion confronts him. And he is deserted.

"But the Lord stood at my side and gave me strength," Paul wrote (2 Timothy 4:17). The ever-present Christ! He is a companion and a remedy for loneliness in our greatest extremity.

We Need Each Other!

Still, it is not his plan that we have no companionship but his. Just as he indwells us, he also indwells every other true believer in the world. We are linked not only to Christ but to those who are Christ's. Whether they like it or not, and whether we like it or not, we are members one of another. We need to reflect that by involving ourselves with others.

Some of them may indeed try to say, "I don't need you." They are wrong. That is not the truth, and we must not reflect the same lie.

"The eye cannot say to the hand, 'I don't need you!' And the head cannot say to the feet, 'I don't need you!' On the contrary, those parts of the body that seem to be weaker are indispensable" (1 Corinthians 12:21-22).

We err when we count anyone as dispensable. Don't consider yourself superfluous, and don't dispense with others. The Lord of the church wants us all.

Relating to others is not just a nice idea. Brotherly kindness is a trait that Scripture commands us to add to our faith.[3] To develop this brotherly love may require that we defy a strong natural pull toward separation. Our every inclination may be to withdraw and nurse our private pain alone.

But to do so would be tragic. Choose brotherhood instead, for it leads to joy.

"How good and pleasant it is when brothers live together in unity!" (Psalm 133:1).

NOTES

1. Whittaker Chambers, *Witness* (New York: Random House, 1952), p. 799.

2. Helmut Thielicke, *Being a Christian When the Chips Are Down* (Philadelphia: Fortress Press, 1979), p. 70.

3. See Stanley C. Baldwin, *How to Build Your Christian Character* (Wheaton, Ill.: Victor Books, 1982) for a discussion of how to add goodness, knowledge, self-control, perseverance, godliness, brotherly kindness, and love to your faith.

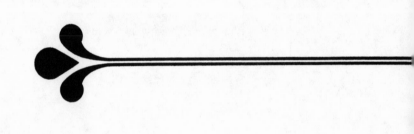

Part 4

Getting on
Top of It All

15
How to Celebrate No Matter What

When Disaster Strikes

What is one of the worst things that could possibly happen to you? Can you bring a specific calamity to mind? Think about it a minute. Now, what would you do if that actually happened? How would you handle it?

Perhaps you don't care much for my questions. You may not want to think about disaster. I can understand that, because I don't like to dwell on negative "what-ifs" either. On the other hand, I don't want to act like a frightened child who won't look under the bed because some menace might be lurking there. I don't want to be so threatened by life's darker possibilities that I can't even contemplate them.

But perhaps your situation is far different. Perhaps you don't need to imagine a "worst thing" happening. You are caught in some ordeal right now, and my asking how you would handle it seems ridiculous. As well talk about handling a tidal wave. Some things you don't handle; the challenge is sheerly to survive.

Believe me, I can understand that feeling, too. Yet I

am here to say that God can give us power to cope with anything that comes into our lives. Anything. In fact, we can do more than cope: We can celebrate!

Not that we can breeze through all our trials laughing, singing, and praising God. If that kind of life can be found anywhere, it's probably among the mentally ill. Such a life certainly cannot be found in the pages of the New Testament.

Jesus wept.

Peter endured enough suffering to write a book about it.

James counseled believers to pray about their afflictions and to endure them patiently.

Paul said it is through much tribulation that we must enter the kingdom, and he described himself as "troubled on every side." He further said that we should weep with those who weep—sharing the pain of others even when our own paths are pleasant (see Romans 12:15).

Nevertheless, as the Prison Epistles reveal, Paul not only had the strength to survive his trials but he also had the grace to rejoice despite his afflictions. He wrote, "Rejoice in the Lord always. I will say it again: Rejoice!" (Philippians 4:4).

Strength to go on and *grace to rejoice*—those are the qualities you and I need when things are tough.

Strength to Go On

Paul was a prisoner when he penned the words that have spoken strength to countless beleaguered Christians: "I can do everything through him who gives me strength" (Philippians 4:13).

I memorized those words as a teenager. I thought I understood them. My grasp of their implications, however, has been expanding ever since. Probably no passage has helped me more in tough times.

When I first became acquainted with Philippians 4:13, it was one of our youth group's memory verses. Even then I almost instinctively knew it was a misuse of the passage for Mary Beth to answer a question about her attendance at the Saturday night skating party by saying simply, "Philippians 4:13." To her it apparently meant she could wangle permission out of her reluctant parents.

Maybe she could. But was that how God intended us to understand and use the verse? I started thinking about it. If I didn't like Mary Beth's use of the verse, how should it be used?

"I can do all things . . ." I let my imagination take over, and it soon went to Superman. Did the verse mean I could leap tall buildings in a single bound? Could I stop a speeding train? Bounce bullets off my chest? Develop x-ray vision?

I decided Philippians 4:13 didn't mean I could literally do anything, no matter how fantastic.

Reading the context helped. Paul had evidently received a gift from the Christians at Philippi. He was glad to get it, but really more pleased with their giving than with his receiving. It showed grace and love on their part, and Paul rejoiced in that. So far as his needs were concerned, he could get along with or without their gift. He could handle being poor and deprived or being prosperous. He could "do all things" through Christ who strengthened him.

This put quite a different light on the verse. It wasn't talking about performing fantastic Superman exploits, but about being able to cope with material adversity or prosperity. To do that was no small accomplishment in itself. My buddy Bill Smith cited a passage from Proverbs that talked about the difficulty of doing that very thing.

> Give me neither poverty nor riches, but give me only my daily bread. Otherwise, I may have too much and disown you and

say "Who is the Lord?" Or I may become
poor and steal, and so dishonor the name
of my God (Proverbs 30:8-9).

Bill felt he was in the same boat with the writer of
Proverbs, and I had to admit I probably was, too. We
agreed that often people couldn't handle poverty and they
couldn't handle wealth, either. Through Christ, Paul
could do both.

While the verse sprang from a money context, however, it seemed to apply more broadly. No doubt the
Christ who strengthened Paul to handle want or plenty
also strengthened him to handle other tests in whatever
form they came. It seemed Paul was claiming to be an adequate person—equal to whatever might come in his life.
In other words, Paul knew how to cope no matter what.

That's why I asked you at the beginning of this chapter to contemplate the worst thing that could happen to
you and to think about how you would handle it.

The Testing Times

Most parents will likely identify with me when I say
that some of my own toughest times have come when my
children have been threatened. How I have needed the
strength of Christ to "do all things" then!

I vividly recall such an incident. I had reached a point
where I already had about all I could handle . . . and then
the *coup de grâce* fell.

My study load by itself had been heavy enough that
summer. Such strange-sounding subjects: Phonetics,
Phonemics, Morphology, Syntax. My wife Marge and I
were at the Summer Institute of Linguistics in Grand
Forks, North Dakota, taking our first tentative steps toward becoming missionary Bible translators.

We had left our infant son Steve back home in Oregon in care of an aunt and uncle. Kathy and Krystal, our

little sweetheart daughters aged three and two, were with us.

I was sick a lot that summer with a severe sore throat. At first I assumed it was "just a cold." But as it recurred with greater intensity and accompanying high fever, the sore throat became more and more puzzling and disturbing. I ended up in the infirmary for care and diagnostic tests.

"Have you ever had malaria?" our head nurse Trudy asked.

"No."

"Ever lived in the tropics, or even visited there?"

"No."

"Have you had scarlet fever?"

"No, but I was inoculated for it in Canada about three years ago, and ever since my left wrist has tended to sweat."

Trudy smiled. No, she didn't think that was significant.

Slowly the sore throat got better and I was released from the infirmary. A few days later it came time for our first in a series of inoculations required for Jungle Camp. Trudy gave us our shots one Saturday morning about nine o'clock. Marge then took Kathy with her for a trip into town, and I took Krystal with me for a brief stopover at the campus library.

I'd been at the library only a few minutes when I noticed Krystal was clenching her teeth and shivering. "Do you have to go potty?" I asked. She didn't reply but continued the strange behavior. I took her to the bathroom and sat her on the stool. She just sat there shaking, and it was obvious something was wrong.

But nothing to get very worried about, I thought. I knew where Trudy was; I'd just trot Krystal back over to her office and let her solve this little mystery.

I was hardly prepared for Trudy's reaction.

"Anaphylactic shock!" she cried out almost immediately. "She's having a reaction to the shots." In a flash Trudy was on the phone to the municipal hospital. "Anaphylactic shock," I heard her say. "We are bringing her in."

The seriousness of the situation still hadn't dawned on me. Our little sweetheart was the picture of health. Strong, happy, good-natured, a bit on the chubby side, she was the light of our lives. Kathy, our firstborn, was the classic beauty, but Krystal with her characteristic scowl at strangers and strange situations, her vulnerability, her complete trust in us, her goodness—Krystal had completely captured our hearts.

But now . . . in minutes she had been stricken, and I didn't grasp it yet. Whatever was wrong, it couldn't be serious. Wasn't Trudy right there to treat her as required? Even the quickly arranged trip to the hospital was reassuring. We'd have all the resources of medical science taking care of this little problem.

While enroute in the car, however, Trudy said something that let me know how things really were. "You'd better pray," she said. "Really pray. This reaction causes spasms—a sort of temporary paralysis. That's why her jaw's set. The spasms will pass, but . . . but meanwhile, if they reach her bronchial tubes, she wouldn't be able to breathe."

So I prayed. I begged God for the life of my little girl. And then, suddenly, a great weakness and weariness swept over me. I had borne the long, heavy studies. I had endured the protracted bout of sickness, from which I was still recovering. I had put up with this muggy, mosquito-infested place half a continent away from my home and my son. But to lose Krystal—that would be too much.

"I couldn't bear it, Lord," I cried. "You've got to save her!"

Then we were at the hospital. Krystal was quickly hooked to an intravenous apparatus. Marge arrived a few minutes later. She brought with her a little box of raisins—our usual treat for the girls—and something else very special, a Hershey bar. Krystal had tasted very little chocolate in her life, and how she loved it!

But now she lay so still and small in her bed that the raisins and the Hershey bar only served to emphasize how sick she was. The little eyes that would have glowed with delight were closed. The chubby fingers that would have dug to the bottom of the raisin box or clutched the chocolate so tightly lay curled and impassive.

Again I implored God to let her live.

He did. The crisis passed quickly and that evening we were able to take Krystal home. The next day she was as good as new. A few days later at a fellowship meeting, Trudy rose to say what an inspiration to her my patience in suffering had been. She knew—better than any of the others—what I had gone through with my own illness and with Krystal.

I was pleased, of course, but I knew something Trudy didn't. I knew I had been ready to break.

Learning to Cope

We never did become foreign missionaries (Krystal's reaction to the shots was only one of the reasons). I did serve as a pastor for some years, and then as a writer, editor, and speaker.

Twenty-seven years after the Grand Forks episode, I was scheduled to conduct a series of meetings for a large church in the Tri-Cities area of Washington state. Krystal had two little girls of her own by then and lived with her husband Bill and family in Moses Lake, Washington. We lived in the Portland area. Tri-Cities lay between the two, so the meeting gave us a great opportunity to get together.

One of the messages I planned to give was "How to Cope No Matter What." But could I cope, really, *no matter what?* Did I dare make such a claim? What if God let Satan put me to the test, like Job? What if he gave me a chance to prove I could cope? Did I want to risk provoking such a test?

I don't mean to suggest that I thought I was putting Krystal at risk, that he might test me again through her. No, any number of things could happen to me—things I couldn't even imagine. The Old Testament tells how God took away the reason of King Nebuchadnezzar to deal with his arrogance. The man went insane. The story concludes with a trenchant warning to all of us: "Those who walk in pride he is able to humble" (Daniel 4:37).

To suggest that I could cope no matter what *did* sound a bit arrogant. And yet there was Philippians 4:13: "I can do everything through him who gives me strength." Wasn't this Paul's testimony while he was in prison that he could cope no matter what?

So I preached it. I took Marge along for the meetings, Krystal and her family came down from Moses Lake, and we all had a marvelous time. The people received my message warmly. No calamity ensued to "teach me a lesson," and I felt sure I had "rightly divided" the Word.

Becoming Self-Sufficient

Some time later my friend John Wilkinson called and invited me to serve as devotional speaker at the annual men's Steelhead Fishing Retreat at Tapawingo in the Oregon Coast Range. "Talk to them about being *the adequate man,*" an inner voice said. I studied Philippians 4:13 and its context again to see if God would say something different to me or confirm what I had found before.

There was little question about it. Paul was claiming cope-ability. But wait. What was this other line in the context? "I have learned to be content whatever the circumstances" (v. 11).

Content? Did Paul mean he was perfectly satisfied to have it that way? Even when he was actually hungry and in want? His two self-descriptions seem almost contradictory. If you are *content,* you don't *want* anything. And if you are hungry, you are not content—at least not with your diet.

What did Paul mean by this word, *content?* How can the original be literally translated? "I for learned in what conditions I am self-sufficient to be." The word *content* literally means *self-sufficient.*

I dug out my Greek-English lexicon. The word in question is *autarkes,* and it occurs only once in Scripture— here, in Philippians 4:11. The prefix, *aut,* means *self.* Just like some familiar English words—*aut*omobile ("self-moving"), *aut*obiography (a story about oneself). The *arkes* stem means *enough* or *sufficient.*

Paul wasn't saying that he was content; he was saying he had been made sufficient to handle whatever might come.

But why wasn't it translated that way? I checked several versions. Only one of them, the New American Standard Bible, introduced this *self-sufficient* idea, and then only in a marginal note. Why? Maybe I could guess . . . "I'm self-sufficient" sounds so arrogant! And I had thought my milder Tri-Cities message, "How to Cope No Matter What" might sound pompous.

Was it arrogance for Paul—and by extension for us— to claim total self-sufficiency? To make such a claim apart from the indwelling Christ certainly would be.

But we are not apart from Christ.

Never, under any circumstances, will he leave us or forsake us. I checked the Greek interlinear Bible for verse 13 and read, "All things can I do *in the one empowering me.*"

My mind went back to J. J. Ray, a salty Sunday school missionary I'd known years before. Praying at a formal church dedication, he shocked some of the crowd by saying, "Lord, I know you are here with us today, for I brought you with me when I came."

While one might have wished for a little more recognition of our corporate standing as the temple of God, J. J. was right. Christ actually indwells us who believe in him. How often Paul had said as much in the Prison Epistles! But I had missed it. Now I seemed to see it everywhere.

Paul prayed that we believers might know "the immeasurable greatness of his power *in us* who believe" (Ephesians 1:19, RSV).

He prayed that we might "be filled to the measure of all the fullness of God," and then immediately declared that God "is able to do immeasurably more than all we ask or imagine, according to his power that is *at work within us*" (Ephesians 3:19-20).

Paul wrote that this Christ-in-you concept was formerly a mystery—"hidden for ages and generations but is now . . . disclosed to the saints" (Colossians 1:26-27). The sad thing is that the reality of Christ in us is still hidden from many of the saints. We simply haven't grasped that we have God's *power* in us because we have *God* in us. That's the glorious message!

Designed for Power

Some time ago my son Steve brought me a Subaru station wagon to advertise and sell for him. I noticed that when I drove the thing, it was gutless. It could hardly make it up Mile Hill coming out to our place from town.

I didn't know if something was wrong with the car or if that was simply characteristic of Subarus. A friend called to ask that same question. "I just overhauled a Subaru," he said. "It seems to run okay now, but it's powerless. Is something wrong with it? Or is that normal for a Subaru?"

I still don't know whether Subarus are built for

power. But I do know about Christians. Believers can tap the limitless power of their Creator, and something is wrong if we lug down and barely make it up life's hills.

Paul was self-sufficient because he drew on the power of the indwelling Christ. He was a self-contained unit. He carried all the resources he needed right inside of him, and therefore he was equal to whatever came. That sufficiency is what we all have in Christ!

Grace to Rejoice

I have faced a few tough times since learning that I'm self-sufficient in Christ. The truth is I haven't always handled them with great ease.

I remember another difficult episode, another child, another hospital. Greg, our youngest, was eighteen when he crashed my motorcycle at highway speed into the side of a pickup truck that pulled in front of him. He could easily have been killed (and without a helmet probably would have been). As it was, he shattered his left knee, broke his wrist, and suffered many cuts and bruises.

Within a few days his knee had been surgically reconstructed and he was back home recuperating. We had all handled the trauma fairly well. But the worst was yet to come.

One week after the accident, Greg was seized with excruciating pain deep in his chest. It was about eleven P.M. Our urgent calls to the doctor brought reassuring words. "Probably just a muscle spasm, but bring him in."

Bring him in? Easily said, but it turned out to be almost impossible to do. Picture a big, strapping fellow more than six feet tall and weighing in excess of 180 pounds. His left leg is in a splint and he can hardly move for the pain. What do you do?

We had no choice but to call an ambulance out from town to our country home. Whoever dispatched the ambulance called our nearby fire department, too, and in moments emergency rescue arrived.

How reassuring! They got Greg on oxygen right away and were soon monitoring heart, blood pressure, and pulse. When the ambulance arrived, strong hands carried Greg on a stretcher to the vehicle's open doors. I rode along in the back with my son, while his mother followed in our car.

The attendant made radio contact with the emergency room, described Greg's vital signs, and communicated our estimated time of arrival. And then we were there.

A preliminary diagnosis indicated not a muscle spasm but a pulmonary embolism—a blood clot in the lungs. A clot had detached from somewhere in the body, probably the knee, and had lodged in the lung. Although this sometimes happens after surgery, it was rare, and especially in a patient so young.

The doctors administered anticoagulents to dissolve the clot and reduce the chance of more emboli. Greg would have to stay in the hospital at least a week. Because the anticoagulant would increase his risk of internal bleeding, even after he came home he would have to avoid riding in a car or doing anything that might cause injury. Otherwise he could bleed to death.

It was after two A.M. when Marge and I finally left the hospital and went home to bed. At five A.M. the phone rang. The nurse said Greg was asking for us.

When we reached his bedside, he had some hard questions. Why had all this happened to him? Was he such a terrible sinner? And why didn't God answer his prayers? He had prayed and prayed not to go through the pain and indignity of being catherized again, as he had been during his previous hospilization. His praying hadn't done any good.

I read to him from Hebrews 12. "Endure hardship as

discipline; God is treating you as sons. For what son is not disciplined by his father?" (v. 7). "God disciplines us for our good, that we may share in his holiness" (v. 10).

His mother talked to him about his relationship with the Lord. He had been going his own way and the Lord wanted him to change directions, to follow him.

After we talked awhile, Marge left the room. Greg had been given another pain pill and was trying to sleep. I sat there in a chair and listened to the words of the Scripture I had read as they reechoed in my mind. I didn't know how much or little the words had meant to Greg, but they surely hit home with me. "What son is not disciplined by his father?"

Greg had been our baby, eight years younger than his closest sibling, and he'd been spoiled. I'd gotten soft in my "old age." I'd never demanded enough from this kid, and now it was too late to do what I should have done earlier. Greg was legally of age and could pretty much do as he pleased.

If I hadn't disciplined him . . . God would.

My lack of sleep, the tension of Greg's illness, the spiritual struggle, my compassion for Greg's suffering— all this, combined with a sense of guilt, overcame me emotionally and I sat there in my chair and wept.

"I can do all things . . ."

"How to cope no matter what . . ."

"The adequate person . . ."

"Self-sufficient . . ."

I ask you: What kind of man sat there in that hospital room, weeping as gray dawn ushered in a new day (a Sunday, no less)? An adequate man? Or a broken one?

I can tell you it was really a man who, though needing an emotional release, was deep inside possessed of incredible strength. There's a difference, you see, between emotional/physical strength and spiritual strength. The former can be exhausted (and often is), but the latter comes in boundless supply. It is Christ in us, and not even our own guilt can drain that strength. Why? He indwells us by grace!

A Reason to Celebrate

We can celebrate that grace no matter what. Even if the worst happens and then that worst is twice compounded by our own behavior, we still have Christ within.

Always, whether at our best or our worst, we stand before him by grace. Always he indwells us. Always he is there to strengthen us.

I don't know any better reason to rejoice. Oh, it's great to rejoice when we've won. It's gratifying to know we've done well. We've met the tests, made the right choices, triumphed over our circumstances. But we don't always win, and we hardly ever score 100 percent. It is then that we can rejoice in God's grace. We can praise God that he doesn't desert us when we are down. He doesn't become a remote God—*up there* or *out there* somewhere, but no longer *here* in our hearts.

This is something we need to understand. In doing so, we are "strengthened . . . to have great endurance and patience." And we are lifted, "joyfully giving thanks to the Father" (Colossians 1:11-12).

Still Celebrating in Old Age

One of my most recent opportunities to preach the great truths about the indwelling Christ came at a Presbyterian church in Santa Clara, California. After the service, an elderly gentleman approached me and said, "I almost got up to interrupt you during your message." His unsmiling, intense manner made me think I was about to get blasted with scathing criticism.

"I am eighty-nine years old," he continued. "I discovered Philippians 4:13 only one year ago, and it has changed my life. When you were preaching I wanted to jump up and tell everyone, 'It's really true, folks!'"

I learned that this man had been a churchgoer most of his life, but was eighty-eight years old before he discovered the dynamic of Christ's power within him. He told me that all his life he had been a stammerer. He tried scores of remedies but nothing helped much.

That is, until he experienced the power of the indwelling Christ. His stammering disappeared.

"And guess what," he said excitedly, "I recently joined Toastmasters and I'm learning public speaking."

Isn't that great? Ah, to be celebrating life at age eighty-nine. That's for me!

Still, I must confess that there are times even now when I don't cope well. They come when I forget the strength and power available to me. It's easy to get your eyes so fixed on the problem that you can't see your inner resources.

Peter knew that. Even after walking on water, he began to sink when he focused on the howling wind and the foaming waves around him.

At such times, however, it takes only a word from Jesus to lift us above the circumstances once again. That word so many times has come from Philippians 4:13.

Paul could do all things through Christ.

I, too, can do all things through Christ.

An eighty-nine-year-old former stammerer in Santa Clara can do all things through Christ.

What about you?